Praise for *The Ministry of Ordinary Places*

"Shannan knows life is about who we are truly *with*. I'm so glad she wrote it all down for us. This book is for EVERYONE. You will love it!"

—Bob Goff, *New York Times* bestselling author
of *Love Does* and *Everybody, Always*

"This is the book we all need right now. If you're longing for authentic community but aren't sure where to begin, Shannan and this beautifully written book are the perfect guide. I truly believe when we stand together we stand a chance. I cheered along with every word."

—Korie Robertson, *New York Times* bestselling author

"This is a message the world needs. So often we overcomplicate 'service' or this elusive call to ministry when all the while ministry is right in front of us. Shannan reminds us of the simple, yet beautiful call to love our neighbor and what that could really look like today. We are reminded that extravagant love in ordinary moments does indeed lead to an extraordinary life."

—Katie Davis Majors, *New York Times* bestselling
author of *Kisses from Katie*

"These are the days when we could all use a firm but gentle nudge to extend extra kindness to the people around us. Shannan reminds us to pay attention, look outside of ourselves, to lay aside our preconceived judgments, and stay put, bearing with each other, carrying each other's burdens, and finding Jesus at the center of it all."

—LaTasha Morrison, founder of Be the Bridge

"Our nonstop consumer society seduces us into forsaking the ordinary. Even as believers, we are prone to aspire to do sexy ministry that garners headlines and warrants photo ops. But Shannan Martin helps us resist these impulses by calling the body to reclaim the sanctity and significance of ordinary places. Through personal stories, theology, and Scripture, she helps us discern God's call upon our lives right where we are and illuminates why the most faithful ministry is oftentimes mundane, overlooked, and seemingly unimpressive. This book will help you thrive in your faith in practical and rooted ways!"

—Dominique DuBois Gilliard, author of *Rethinking Incarceration: Advocating for Justice That Restores*

"Sometimes when reading a book, I think 'I'll recommend this to that group' or 'this one goes go that community,' but hand to heaven, I would put this book in every single pair of hands across ideology, camps, and tribes. Part storytelling, part prophetic, with dizzyingly wonderful writing, Shannan brings us back to the neighborhood, back to ordinary tables, back to a life we know in our deepest hearts is meant for us. I love her. I love this book."

—Jen Hatmaker, *New York Times* bestselling author of *7*, *For the Love*, and *Of Mess and Moxie*

"'I was terrified of being ordinary,' and with that one sentence Shannan Martin sums up every single one of us. Certainly me. And then she deconstructs the cliché of ordinary and puts it back together with pictures and stories and sidewalks full of people who will make you want to cry or sing or despair or dance or rail or just quietly whisper, amen. This book is a new pair of eyes. Go ahead, open them!"

—Lisa-Jo Baker, bestselling author of *Never Unfriended* and *Surprised by Motherhood*

"Photographers often talk about the 'golden hour' of each day—the hour just before the sun slips beyond the horizon. The light, they tell us, is perfect, then. You've probably seen it? All of everything around us seems to glow with the murmur of heaven—the streetlights, the graffiti on the walls, the rainbow'd puddles of oil-slicked water and the golden heads of wheat that bow to a gentle breeze. In these pages, Shannan Martin places a gentle hand on our shoulder and whispers quiet and profound words of truth, telling us the golden hour is here—right now—with these people in this place at this moment. Now. Heaven is all around us, and this book invites us, as only Shannan can, to awaken to a life where every ordinary moment shimmers with gold."

—Deidra Riggs, author, speaker, disco-lover

"In a world where hope seems dim and solutions feel complicated and partisan, Shannan Martin offers us a starting point that is as radical as it is domestic: widen your circle, hush your mouth, and *pay close attention*. This book is the right book for this moment in time and I simply cannot get over it. I either laughed or cried on almost every page. We need these lyrical, prophetic words now more than ever before."

—Emily P. Freeman, *Wall Street Journal* bestselling author of *Simply Tuesday*

"Through ordinary stories of mustard seeds, lost coins, and surly prodigals, Jesus taught that the kingdom of God has come near and we are called to be its ambassadors in our everyday lives. In the tradition of Jesus and all the best storytellers, Shannan uses her ordinary, beautiful, oh-so-relatable life to show us that we are called to embody the love of God in our communities and that God has equipped us with everything we need to be ministers right where we are. Full of grace, humor, and kindness, Shannan makes you believe that your voice, your gifts, your perspective are so needed to help mend our broken world, proclaiming that yes, even now, the kingdom of God has come near."

—Osheta Moore, author of *Shalom Sistas*

"*The Ministry of Ordinary Places* tears down the high and mighty calling we've often conjured in our minds about how the faithful serve God and instead invites us to see a sacred call in the faces of our neighbors, to smell the holy incense in ashtrays filled with crooked cigarette butts, or to see the broken bread set before us in a Burger King table for two. Shannan challenges who our neighbor is then offers a glimpse of what it might look like to stay put, stick around, and find that our best life is one where we simply pay attention to that common ache to be known and seen and loved, just as we are. In a book that's both challenging and down to earth, she leads us into a theology of ordinary places, of neighborliness, secondhand smoke, and the holy ground of discovering our way home is always together."

—Alia Joy, author of *Glorious Weakness: Discovering God in All We Lack*

"Shannan's brilliance and grace invites us into the narrow way of Jesus, a path beyond walls, borders, and fences. God met me in fresh and unexpected ways through this book, and I believe He'll do the same for you."

—Rebekah Lyons, author of *You Are Free* and *Freefall to Fly*

the
ministry
of
ordinary places

the
ministry
of
ordinary places

WAKING UP TO GOD'S GOODNESS AROUND YOU

SHANNAN MARTIN

NELSON
BOOKS

An Imprint of Thomas Nelson

Published in Nashville, Tennessee, by Nelson Books, an imprint of Thomas Nelson. Nelson Books and Thomas Nelson are registered trademarks of HarperCollins Christian Publishing, Inc.

Published in association with Yates & Yates (www.yates2.com).

The names and identifying characteristics of some of the individuals featured throughout this book have been changed to protect their privacy.

Thomas Nelson titles may be purchased in bulk for educational, business, fund-raising, or sales promotional use. For information, please e-mail SpecialMarkets@ThomasNelson.com.

Scripture quotations are taken from *Holy Bible*, New Living Translation. © 1996. Used by permission of Tyndale House Publishers, Inc., Wheaton, Illinois 60189. All rights reserved.

Any Internet addresses, phone numbers, or company or product information printed in this book are offered as a resource and are not intended in any way to be or to imply an endorsement by Thomas Nelson, nor does Thomas Nelson vouch for the existence, content, or services of these sites, phone numbers, companies, or products beyond the life of this book.

ISBN 978-0-7180-7749-5 (eBook)

Library of Congress Cataloging-in-Publication Data
Names: Martin, Shannan, 1976- author.
Title: The ministry of ordinary places : waking up to God's goodness around you / Shannan Martin.
Description: Nashville : Thomas Nelson, 2018. | Includes bibliographical references.
Identifiers: LCCN 2018005119 | ISBN 9780718077488
Subjects: LCSH: Love--Religious aspects--Christianity.
Classification: LCC BV4639 .M3264 2018 | DDC 248.4--dc23 LC record available at https://lccn.loc.gov/2018005119

Printed in the United States of America
18 19 20 21 22   PC/LSCH   10 9 8 7 6 5 4 3

For my neighbors. You are my moon in the morning, reflecting Jesus and taking me by surprise. I will always search the sky for you.

"If you look for me wholeheartedly, you will find me. I will be found by you," says the LORD.

—Jeremiah 29:13–14

The heavens proclaim the glory of God.
    The skies display his craftsmanship.
Day after day they continue to speak;
    night after night they make him known.
They speak without a sound or word;
    their voice is never heard.
Yet their message has gone throughout the earth,
    and their words to all the world.

—Psalm 19:1–4

Contents

CONTENTS

PART FOUR: LOVE SONG FOR THE LONG HAUL

The Call

I always thought being called by God was a rare and special thing that happened to only a slim percentage of unlucky people.

I'm just being honest.

When I heard proclamations of someone going into "full-time ministry" (as opposed to occasional or intermittent ministry, I guess), I assumed the unfortunate soul would end up in one of two places: the church on the corner with a high turnover rate or a developing country overseas. I don't know what it says about me—and I had friends who felt otherwise, pining to be chosen—but both options made me shiver.

This low-grade anxiety over whether or not I would be "called" by God ebbed and flowed even into adulthood. I was unable to shake the feeling that it was still possible. Whenever it popped up, I kindly reminded God that I'm not that kind of woman. I'm indoorsy, with a sensitive gag reflex and a mortal phobia of outhouses. I'm not the best choice for a day trip to a state park, much less the mission field.

All along, I viewed ministry as something to be avoided. When my sturdy, athletic younger sister moved to Zambia to be a missionary, I knew I was home free. *Bullet dodged.*

At last, I put my irrational ministry fears behind me and got to work on the task at hand, which for me was mothering. I maneuvered my babies into sleep schedules, taught them to pray, and took them to the library often. I had found my calling. It wasn't *all of that* after all. It was *this right here*, this thing in front of me.

Like every generation before me, I blazed a trail through those early, chaotic years of motherhood, realizing along the way, almost accidentally, that as my kids were getting older, the burden on me was lessening. I am as wildly in love with them as I have ever been. I still creep into their rooms most nights to watch them sleeping, as this remains the most reliable antidote to most crimes against motherhood and is, in general, an excellent way to wrap up even the blue ribbon days. But as they began needing me less and in different ways, I started to realize that maybe caring for them wasn't the full extent of my calling.

I went about my life believing God had more plans for me, wrought with mystery and nuance, hidden just outside my line of vision. Quite honestly, it was easier to soldier forward in my pursuit of being a good, Christian woman and just hope it would all shake out in the wash. I signed Calvin up for kindergarten, taught Ruby to tie her shoes, and potty trained Silas for what seemed like thirteen years. I learned to bake bread from scratch. I planted flowers and, on the best of days, I blow-dried my hair. I joined a Bible study at church, wrote out a budget, and tithed each month. I read books, stayed up on the news, and listened to Christian radio.

It worked for a while, until it all fell apart. I lost much of what I'd fought to hold, like my American, middle-class versions of security, safety, and comfort. After imagining the foreseeable decades of our life pinned flat and even like the squares of a quilt, my husband, Cory, and I were stunned to realize that God was asking for more from us, and it was going to look like less. In short order we unexpectedly lost our prestigious government jobs and a large chunk of the savings account we had coddled like our extra child. God asked us to surrender the farmhouse we loved and the small-town life where we fit right in and instead move to a neighborhood on the wrong side of the tracks, a city away, where we knew no one.

It seemed improbable, us, an urban family. I was a blogger known as Flower Patch Farmgirl, my identity so attached to the white fence around our quaint home that I struggled to imagine myself apart from it. But with very little life experience to carry us into this unexpected detour, we grabbed hands and jumped. With a good bit of old-fashioned fear in our bellies, we flung ourselves into both the low-income public school and the dying church at the end of our street. We were sure that's what God was asking of us, though the *why* and *how* remained hazy.

Somewhere on the path toward the weird way of Jesus, where conventional wisdom is replaced with foolish love and unpopular alliances, I uncovered my calling. It wasn't new. It had always been there. But now, I was ready to see it. And because I'm your friend to the end, I'm here to save you the trouble: it's your calling too.

As Christ-followers, we are called to be long-haul neighbors committed to authenticity and willing to take some risks. Our vocation is to invest deeply in the lives of those around us, devoted to one another, physically close to each other as we breathe the same air and walk the same blocks. Our purpose is not so mysterious after all. We get to love and be deeply loved right where we're planted, by whomever happens to be near. We will inevitably encounter brokenness we cannot fix, solve, or understand, and we'll feel as small, uncertain, and outpaced as we have ever felt. But we'll find our very lives in this calling, to be among people as Jesus was, and it will change everything.

The details will look quiet and ordinary.

They will exhaust and exhilarate us.

But it will be the most worth-it adventure we will ever take.

Let's go.

Part One

The Lost Art of Paying Attention

Chapter One

Who Even *Is* My Neighbor?

I sat at the pint-sized table at the coffee shop downtown, my knees banging against its worn wooden edge each time I shifted in my seat. Across from me sat my dear friend Becca. Her hands were wrapped around a mug of coffee, probably something exotic like Sumatra or Ethiopian blend, all direct trade, naturally. But Becca doesn't particularly care about the origins of her beans, and I'm a tea-drinking contrarian. The coffee was never the point.

Conversation percolated around us, bubbling up now and then into laughter among women flushed and limber from morning yoga, stay-at-home dads with strollers, city leaders, freelancers, and tunnel-visioned students. An orthodox priest in a floor-length black robe took the table to our left, and to our right sat two men knitting, one of whom wore a bun. Right in the middle sat the two of us, me hiding yesterday's hair under my signature red ball cap, and Becca wearing a sweatshirt decorated with an airbrushed, wintry landscape.

As usual, we were trying to figure out how to fix the world.

It wouldn't be unfair to classify this assemblage of two opinionated verbal processors as a glorified vent session, with plenty of comic relief mixed in. We were both political junkies (recovering and otherwise), so the upcoming presidential election was foremost on our minds, and the fact that we didn't agree on a solution only added punch to our discussion. On top of that we were both experiencing near-terminal church-related funk, the racial tension of our country continued to be revealed, religious people were damning each other to hell over a legion of issues, and there were new rumblings that we might be on the brink of war. It was a lot.

Along the way, Becca elevated the emotional atmosphere with stories about her former cough-drop-addicted house pig named Brats and her misadventures involving an accordion. When one of us rambled, the other went up for air, taking a sip of our now lukewarm beverages, careful not to miss a word. These coffee dates were not for the faint of heart, which presented a problem since Becca had been clinically diagnosed with a mouthful of medical jargon amounting to "faint of heart." As always, we tried to keep our cool.

Becca and I first met at the little Methodist church my family attends. Fueled by mutual intrigue and maybe a bit of shared loneliness, we graduated from Sunday handshakes to these intermittent Wednesday mornings.

Separated by twenty-five years, the two of us were never meant to be friends and certainly not coconspirators. She is a single woman with no children and a senior discount. I'm young enough to be her daughter. Our ideologies don't perfectly align. Our theologies tear away from each other now and then. Yet, in each other, we recognized the reward of stepping outside our norm, and our unlikely friendship grew. Before long, we were neighbors of the city and the heart, and, if I know anything at all, it's that the route leading from "neighbor" to "family" is surprisingly short. I never imagined myself with a friend like Becca, someone I would come to depend on in meaningful ways. And, yet, here we were. It wasn't hard at all.

Time after time, we circle back to a few key questions: *Why is this world so messed up? Why does God choose to fiddle around with the likes of us? What on earth can we do to make this sad and beautiful world a little softer for everyone?*

I can't say that we often walk away from our time together with clear answers or solutions. But I always walk away feeling more hopeful. This is the promise of Emmanuel, God with us, who came near in body and stayed in Spirit. It's no accident that the solace of eternity is so often parceled out in one-hour chunks and passed around the table.

I know you're right there with me and Becca at that tiny table, nodding along. We believe God hasn't forgotten us and that he has a plan to renew the beauty lost in the weeds. We are mothers, daughters, sisters, and friends. We want the younger generations to thrive in a new way. We want the older generations to feel seen, heard, and valued. We're no longer satisfied with a solution that only serves us and those like us. We want a plan that serves the whole sisterhood, stretching beyond bloodlines and the culture that for too long has pitted us against each other.

Where we've been taught to self-protect, we're now ready to reach out, not just to people who remind us of ourselves, but to anyone in arm's reach. We're ready to lean in. We're just not sure how to start.

Though our lives feel ordinary and small, we're compelled by the possibility of making a difference where the problems loom large. We want to offer the hope of Christ in a world that feels increasingly fractured and gloomy. We believe we can be world shakers from our own little corners, where there are crumbs on the floor and no righteous plan for the dinner hour barreling toward us. We're growing desperate to experience the mess of the gospel, trading our tight reins and safe ways for the mystery and mayhem of God's kingdom making its way down.

It's all too easy to lose our purpose in the details of everyday life: the leftovers, the empty gas tank, the meetings that run too long. We know we're called to love our neighbor, but we're leery of risk. We come from a long line of social awkwardness.

And, anyway, who even *is* our neighbor?

In Luke 10, we peer in on a Jewish expert of religious law unwisely trying to trick Jesus. After an intense volley of smug superiority (Jewish guy) and the sort of composed calm guaranteed to rattle even the most seasoned debater (Jesus), the man asks the same question we're asking, "And who is my neighbor?" (v. 29).

In classic Jesus fashion, his answer comes in story form. In this parable, a Jewish man mugged, bloodied, and left for dead on the Jericho road is rescued not by a Jewish priest or a temple assistant, both of whom saw him and kept walking, but by a Samaritan. The Jewish people loathed Samaritans, considering them half-bred lowlives. Yet it was he, the unlikeliest ally, who "felt compassion" for the wounded Jewish man, daubing his wounds, hoisting him onto his donkey, holding him steady along that winding road, emptying his pockets for the Jewish man's care, and pledging his help until healing came.

Through this parable, we don't hear a single word from the injured Jewish man's perspective. We don't know what he was thinking or how he responded. We aren't allowed the satisfaction of him weeping in gratitude or apologizing to his rescuer for the rocky history between their people. We don't know if he received assistance with humility or if he choked back the judgment still coursing through him, just happy to be alive. Simply put, we don't know if the merciful encounter with his sworn enemy changed him. It's hard to believe it wouldn't have, but that isn't the point here.

The story is centered on the Samaritan, the one who had everything to lose, who couldn't bear to see someone hurting and dared to get involved. Though it certainly cost him, he chose the neighbor way.

In Dr. Martin Luther King Jr.'s historic "I've Been to the Mountaintop" speech, given the day before his assassination, he said of the parable, "The question is not, 'If I stop to help this man in need, what will happen to me?'" Rather, it is, what will become of our bloodstained neighbor if we choose to pass by instead? "What will happen to them?" Dr. King asked the crowd. "That's the question."[1]

Who is my neighbor?

It's not the one who looks like me. It's not the one I am most comfortable with or the one with whom I share hobbies, talents, or a go-to Starbucks order. It's not limited to the person next door or my favorite coworker. My neighbor might even be someone I despise.

My neighbor is the one who comes near in mercy.

My neighbor is the one to whom *I* draw near in mercy.

At times I am the Jewish man, with my insider status, skepticism, and, despite it all, my deep, immediate need. Other times, I am the Samaritan man, taking a risk by getting myself mixed up in the mess of someone's life when it would be easier to keep my distance. As I see myself in both men, the two-way street of kinship unfolds in front of me.

This invites some careful thought. Life is pulsing around us, waving us closer. Who, then, are we *with*?

Living an on-the-ground, available-and-engaged, concerned-for-our-neighbors lifestyle doesn't necessarily require moving, downsizing, changing jobs, or adopting a child. It only asks that we view our immediate world with fresh eyes to see how we might plant love with intention and grit. This means we'll have to unlearn what we've wrongly absorbed about who people are and what they deserve. We'll have to scratch through the surface and get down to the roots of the stories playing out in our midst. We will have to choose to widen our circle and allow our lives to become tangled up with those around us.

There at the coffee shop, amid our questions, anecdotes,

and rants, what Becca and I were really asking was, *How can we help?* and, *What do I have to offer this cynical world?*

For Becca, the journey toward intentional action began with seeing her knack for storytelling as a legitimate spiritual gift meant to fortify the bruised and battered body of Christ. When an opportunity to teach creative writing at the county jail opened up, she defied logic and surmounted the hurdle of self-doubt by simply, magnificently, saying yes.

At the age of sixty-four, she drove her old beater out of the city and into what many see as a wasteland, inviting long-forgotten mamas to reconsider their stories under a new lens of empowerment and purpose. Each Saturday, she sits with them in a windowless room to discuss the life force held in the folds of their personal histories. They are Romans 5:3 in shapeless, beige uniforms, suffering, resilient, growing, and hopeful: *"We can rejoice, too, when we run into problems and trials, for we know that they help us develop endurance."*

Every line extracted from their pain and scripted into fresh journals, every story shared without the threat of condemnation, every tear wept and every joke cracked has fused this haphazard gathering of society's outcasts into an abiding community of support and shared sorrow. As we sat together at the coffee shop, Becca marveled at the resourcefulness of the women— "They bring supplies and hand roll their own tampons while we talk! Have you ever imagined such a thing?"—and choked up at the ways this sacred space has fundamentally reshaped her worldview while she wasn't looking, immersed in simply loving them and being dazzled by their light. She can't fix the problems of drug addiction, broken families, or the plight of shattered confidence, but she can find her place in the lives of a few women and believe that it matters.

Somewhere toward the end of our coffee date, Becca smacked the table with the palm of her hand, and I knew to lean in. "We're paying attention now," she said. "This will change everything."

She's exactly right.

This mission humbly asks that we devote ourselves to the overlooked spiritual practice of paying attention to wherever God has placed us. That's where we begin, and, though it's not terribly complicated, it will ask more of us than we ever imagined.

Becca called early yesterday morning to say her heart was feeling faint again, but the doctors were working on it and she'd hopefully be as good as new for the next writing class.

I spent forty minutes this morning playing Emotional Bingo with an at-risk third grader at the elementary school who, in just two visits, had already mentored me on the ways of acceptance, fortitude, and grape-sharing.

Meanwhile, my husband, Cory, helped orchestrate an emergency bike delivery for a friend looking to be hired at the bacon factory across town, then shared lunch and a game of cards with his friends inside the jail where he works as the chaplain.

These small moments, over time, stack into something much bigger than ourselves. One tiny risk, one inconvenience, one imperceptible nudge after another, and here we are, thick in community among lonely neighbors, cranky neighbors, and neighbors whose love and optimism shine like the sun on our faces. There have been drug-addicted neighbors who drove us straight to the brink with them, and dark days when we watched despair grow fists and teeth and eat them alive. Even still, I couldn't have imagined the way this basic act of really being with the people near us would sweep through our lives like fresh air and impossible beauty.

The loudest revolutions often begin so quietly, so unassumingly near the ground that most don't bother to notice. I won't speak for you, but surrounded by cynics, worrywarts, doomsday prophets, and Facebook apologists with their lofty solutions, I'd rather be a hope-holder with mud on my shoes. We might have a zillion reasons to be jaded about our world, but that is not the kind of person I want to be. I want to be someone who clings to the grace and the gift and the good. Rather than spend my days scanning the digital horizon for a dopamine hit of false comfort, I want to keep my ear tuned to the groanings of my place. I want to stand ready, as Christ's ambassador in my neighborhood, wearing grace, flesh, and skinny jeans. I want to belong, just as I am, and I want to get better at loving people for every good and puzzling thing they are.

The world around us does its best to make us suspicious and wary, but when we stand together, we are closer to hope.

Wide awake and fully present, let's stick around and dig deep.

Who knows what might happen next?

Chapter Two

Locking Eyes with the World We're In

The paint was already flaking off the baseboards before I realized it was time to stop calling our house new.

The signs were everywhere. Mature grass finally blanketed the postage-stamp yard. The tree we'd bought with 2013's tax refund was large enough to produce a spot of shade exactly wide enough for one person to enjoy. And the clincher—we had returned home from an out-of-town trip and the house didn't smell new. Somewhere along the slow rush of time, when we were distracted by other things, the lumber, paint, and drywall had absorbed the precise essence of *us*.

My new reality still took me by surprise.

I had evolved from the fresh-faced farm girl living my version of the American Dream with a side of Jesus. I'd become the gutsy, subversive, city-loving advocate. The new neighbor. My kids went to a new school. We lived in a new house.

On and on it went, my fists closing around this latest rendition of my identity, just as they had before.

But as people came into our lives and left us, as the carpet wore down in the sorry way carpet is prone to disappoint us, it became harder to ignore. We were no longer new. We were just *here*. The headline had faded. The sparkle dimmed.

Our earlier questions—*Where are we going? Why are we going?* and *Will we ever fit in?*—were replaced with just one: *Now what?* Surely God did not lead us here just to *live*. Surely spending our lives for his sake would mean more than attending PTO meetings and allowing the neighbor kids to conspire with ours in tearing up the yard. Wasn't there some grand, specific thing he wanted and needed me to *do* here?

One late August morning, right in the middle of this heightened spiritual unrest, I decided to walk my kids to school rather than driving the short distance. I'm not sure what flipped the switch. It might have been the hissing shame that I was modeling an odd brand of privilege and laziness for my three young kids. But I had seen enough to understand that growth often requires death, and sometimes death looks like losing that extra fifteen minutes of sleep. Sometimes it asks us to surrender our softest pajama pants and lace up our walking shoes for the greater good, even if we're not quite sure why it matters.

We set out with no grand or holy awakening in mind. I simply wanted to be a more positive presence for the three quirky kids who greet each day with gusto and would surely benefit from their mom at least trying to do the same.

And so we began. We walked almost every morning that year. Day after day, my feet traced the path south, then home again. Rain, shine, under what was often still the cover of night and through the driving snow that makes us ask deep, philosophical questions like, "Does summer really exist? And if so, why does it allow winter to happen to good people?" We walked like a small assembly of sturdy postal carriers saddled not with junk mail, but with backpacks, a violin, and widespread concern over the daily cafeteria menu.

I still didn't know what was next for us here on Fifth Street, but my feet had committed a three-block stretch of it to permanent muscle memory. At the point that you instinctively know where the sidewalk buckles like a compound fracture, existential crises about belonging begin to evaporate. Though I enjoyed the slower start to our day, it would take months before I began to see this routine as significant. In what seems to be a defining pattern of my faith, God was disguising his heaviest lifting toward the health of my soul as mundane, repetitive grunt work.

My *Now what?* was answered in the wail of the train, in the whip of the wind, in the storm-weary oak tree jutting like a mangled arrow straight into the sky: *Pay attention.*

Two little words, light on action, or so I thought. I scanned my perimeter, certain the back half of the message had slipped into a mud puddle or gotten lost in the leaves. *Pay attention to what?*

It's not that attentiveness is a bad idea; it's just that I come from a lineage of capable women. We're learners. Triers. I have worked as a waitress and washed cars while wearing a business suit. My second child was born when the first was barely walking, and our third came home with a penchant for inciting calamity on the daily. The fourth arrived fresh from prison, in the middle of Snowpocalypse.

I can make an elaborate risotto with one hand tied to an elementary school reading log. I can keep us stocked in toilet paper and granola bars and make tacos for a small army. Like every woman I know, I can multitask. Wasn't there something I could physically *do* while I, I don't know, looked around with keen interest? *Is that what it means to pay attention, God?*

Our first few years in our neighborhood had proven that love in action is the natural outpouring of the weighty grace we have been given. My joints were still a bit creaky from the impact of this truth. I waited for a to-do list, an ironclad set of instructions, complete with cross-referenced scriptures.

I trusted him to clear a path, then sat shell-shocked when he showed me my seat.

I asked for a shovel, or maybe a hammer. He handed me binoculars and my worn New Balance tennis shoes.

God got busy shrinking the world as I knew it down to a pinhole, one solitary shaft of light. "The soul exists and is built entirely out of attentiveness," wrote Mary Oliver. Rather than feeling stuck in a problem-sodden world I would never be able to fix, God was caring for my soul by pointing me toward my corner of it and asking me to believe it was enough.

For a while, life became uncharacteristically quiet, and I was forced to slow down. I thought about growth patterns, observed the life cycle of decay and rebirth, and drank endless cups of tea. I searched for the story existing on the underarc of everyday life, where sizable change so often goes unseen. I noticed battered things and contemplated shadows, secretly judging God for his questionable time-management skills when there was so much work to be done.

Under the light of each new day, I walked. And I saw.

Back when we left our six-acre Eden, I was terrified the change of address marked the end of beauty for me. (It felt as dramatic as it sounds.) My logic went something like this: Surrounded by soybean fields and wildflowers, every day was an exercise in enjoying God's smashing eye for design. Pulling ourselves out of that frame—the only one I had ever known—it was beyond me to imagine how the joyride might continue. I assumed he would have to repair my wiring, scooping out my longing for beauty like seeds from a pumpkin.

But the air was changing—or maybe it was me—while we made our way south each day. God sent up smoke signals in bizarre plumes of cloud and erected billboards on cluttered porches: *Do you see me here?* Imagine my surprise when, rather than changing my heart that pounds for beauty, God slowly began changing my lenses, restoring my vision to clearly see what he had always intended. The world was waiting to take my breath away.

It shook me one morning when I noticed the moon still hanging among the clouds. A minor obsession was born, and I began searching for it each day. Some mornings it was a low-slung crescent and other times barely visible behind fog thick enough to eat with a spoon. Now and then it was no more than a faint white smudge, as though God had been painting earlier in the day and didn't get around to washing his hands. He leaves evidence of his nearness everywhere, if we're looking. Why not the sky?

Once, we walked alongside the supermoon, pinned seemingly within our reach, large enough to swallow us whole. The moon, I learned, is not itself a source of light, but a reflection of the sun. My youngest son thinks it's a miracle, and I'm inclined to agree. The universe couldn't possibly deliver a more perfect metaphor for a life in close communion with Christ, where we exist not to light our own way but rather to reflect God's glory.

God had my attention each morning in a way he hadn't before. He was right there with me, revealing truth through creation. Attentiveness is prayer breathed at street level, I once heard someone say. I was starting to believe it.

The tangle of power lines I once saw as distracting and ugly were now fingers laced overhead, a comforting picture of connectedness, all of us tied together, strung from the same cord.

Alleys dotted with trash cans, trees in various stages of undress, homes with splitting porch rails and those with fancy landscaping—each sang a different verse from the same song. I saw in them God's most enduring work, which is often the slowest and most invisible to our darting eyes. *Happiness depends on seeing this as beautiful*, I thought, capturing the moment with my phone and letting the truth penetrate my soul.

Some days, we watched ruined things crumble and be hauled away, brick by brick, entire histories left out in the rain. Other days, we settled into our front-row seats for the rebirth. Seasons changed, and we changed with them. Every day became its own kind of spring, good things growing from low places, belonging to everyone, teaching us to stick our necks out, take a risk, and bloom in spite of struggle.

Two years later, this unspectacular, all-weather walk continues to give depth to my desire to love God more and put skin on his command to find kinship among my neighbors. Observing the changing of the seasons, I came to see with certainty that this daily practice was holy, a liturgy cut into busted sidewalks as we followed the clouds and thanked God for the trees. The larger world still felt impossibly complicated and overwhelming. But I was beginning to realize that it wasn't my concern in the first place. Barbara Brown Taylor wrote, "It is not necessary to take on the whole world at first. Just take the three square feet of earth on which you are sitting, paying close attention to everything that lives within that small estate."[1]

Simply put, we cannot love what we do not know.

We cannot know what we do not see.

We cannot see anything, really, until we devote ourselves to the lost art of paying attention.

In Jesus' life we see an active relationship with God and vibrant ministry woven into the fibers of normal daily tasks.

His sandals must have been worn thin with the miles he logged as he lived fully human—working, resting, eating—all while continually drawing those around him into deeper faith. Intimately attuned to his own physical surroundings, his model for discipleship often began not with instructions to hole up and study more, but with a call to greater awareness.

"Taste and see."

"Listen."

"Stay awake."

He sent his followers out, "Go. With your eyes wide open."

The Son lived at the mercy of his Father. The two were intimately connected. Yet the earthly ministry of Jesus was propelled by watchful obedience. He saw. He heard. He paid attention to those who were hungry. He noticed when a frail hand reached out through the crowd to touch the hem of his robe.

The story of Jesus is infused with the scents of perfume, yeast, and the rotting flesh of his beloved friends. It is flavored with the wine of celebration and the salt of tears. His physical senses drew him to his neighbors, forming the common ground of people cultivating this rhythm of togetherness, the essence of shalom.

Slowly, I began to understand that what God was asking of me was indeed a very small thing. In his kingdom economy, most great things are. Today, in a small city in Indiana, I continue to be schooled in the ways of seeing—*really* seeing—my place and her people. This unlikely education is born of repetition, hyperawareness, and the audacity to believe God is already at work around me in the shadows and cracks. After spending decades trying to wave him into my gleaming best efforts, I found him in the chain-link fencing, in the crumbling sidewalks, in the litter, and in all the light.

Catching the glow of God's presence in the humblest of places, everything old seemed new again. I found myself straining to explain why I had gone gaga over what most people would see as rubble. It didn't make sense even to me. Overgrown yards had once earned a hefty eyeroll from me and graffiti was the mark of a misspent youth. It certainly wasn't art. I wasn't used to ratty things compelling me to desire. More often, they made me want to turn away. Why? What was I afraid of?

I know the truth. I know it like I know different truths about oceans and rainbows and an artsy close-up of a perfect latte. I prefer to be seen as special. Unique. Ordinary places and average people remind me of everything I'm pretending not to be.

The worst part about this fruitless mission to outrun ordinary is that sometimes it kind of works. Sometimes, the applause is loud enough to drown out the sound of our souls collapsing under the weight of a burden we were never meant to carry.

All the while, we're peering out our windows, waiting to be seen for exactly who we are. We're walking sidewalks and cereal aisles, longing for the assurance that we have something to offer, that we are worthy of connection and love.

In *The Ragamuffin Gospel*, Brennan Manning wrote,

Jesus says the kingdom of His Father is not a subdivision for the self-righteous nor for those who feel they possess the state secret of salvation. The kingdom is not an exclusive, well-trimmed suburb with snobbish rules about who can live there. No, it is for a larger, homelier, less self-conscious cast of people who understand they are sinners because they have experienced the yaw and pitch of moral struggle.[2]

Jesus chose the clumsy and the common. Like me. Under the yellow lamplight of our first year in the city, I held my breath through Manning's entire book. "The Good News means we can stop lying to ourselves," he wrote. I nearly choked on the rush of relief. Looking out at the unremarkable neighborhood that was growing more stunning to me by the day, circling up with people pushed to the margins of society, his words were a feather in my soul, as Emily Dickinson wrote. They were hope.

Out in the land of the living, clouds unfurl spectacularly, the sun is moody, the air and the stuff it carries wear differently against our faces. There are frosted violets, dipped in the last traces of March's snow. One week later, the forsythia shows up like a favorite, long-lost cousin. Creation enjoys a cellular inability to run from God's glory. In slipping this one corner beneath the microscope, God points a beam of light on who he has always been. In teaching me to invest deeply in this potholed street, he is pulling me to his chest.

Eugene Peterson said, "All theology is rooted in geography."[3] Just a few years ago, I would have missed the meaning.

Now, it's among the surest things I know. God is calling to us from the world we're in. He wants to meet us right here.

My morning liturgy doesn't begin or end on the interior. It's not just prayer, and it's not only paying attention. It's an active chase toward the goodness of God, a living, breathing hunt for the lovely and an impulse to capture it for safekeeping. It's a physical thing, this glory made known within me, not as I sit in silence but as my body moves and my soul stirs. He cannot possibly be ignored. There are mornings I am sure I hear God laughing, that riotous acknowledgment of pure delight, the same laugh he passed on to my friend Holly—a gift to anyone lucky enough to know her. This is what I know of daily quiet time with the Lord. It is often not so quiet after all. It's a ruckus. A sacred inconvenience. A stunning catastrophe, not to be missed. We were not made for the curated image of success and comfort but for the grit and glory of heartbroken humans on trash day.

In a world that pushes us toward bigger, better, more costly and refined, seeing the humble as radiant is an act of holy resistance. Jesus dealt in seeds and sails. He spoke through dust and sermonized in spit. Set against a backdrop of faithlessness, lawlessness, and low-grade despair, he brought faith and healing through the overlooked, unspectacular elements of everyday life. He's right here, in every dull, dusty corner, and even more, in every one of us bumbling, regular, milk-mustached kids trying to masquerade as big shots. This is why we need him near, and why it matters that we stick together.

We welcome into our lives the complicated people doing

their best but finding their own attempts lacking and remember neediness is our birthright. We show up for one another, pounding stakes into the earth we share, claiming our ground as humans who don't want to be unspectacular on our own. This is the alchemy of the ordinary, my humdrum humanity fusing with yours to create something altogether extraordinary. Somehow, crammed together in close proximity, we form a more luminous reflection of God and his wide, weird kingdom.

Isn't it lovely?

When our well-being gets snarled up with the well-being of our neighbors, when we're truly glad for the house with the vast array of lawn ornaments and the loud music only makes us think of dancing, we've found our song. When we carry a mental map of the crumbliest sidewalks and choose to walk them anyway, we will find ourselves at home.

"You know the saying, 'Four months between planting and harvest.' But I say, wake up and look around. The fields are already ripe for harvest" (John 4:35).

These are the words of Jesus, spoken for the disciples and for us.

We are living, breathing contradictions set into haphazard motion from the foundations of the earth. When it comes to ministry, actively sharing God's grace and love with the world, we need a whole lot of help.

But if we're willing to wake up to the world pulsing around us, if we're paying attention, we might be surprised.

We just might catch the moon in the morning.

Chapter Three

Speech Therapy for the Common Big Mouth (Like Me)

Only a month or so after moving to town, a woman rode up to our house on her bike, passing out flyers for an upcoming neighborhood meeting. She was cheerful without trying too hard, down-to-earth, helpful, and friendly. I pegged her at somewhere around my age, though she wore the look of easy youthfulness, like someone who did a lot of yoga or juiced a lot or, I don't know, just generally enjoyed life.

We chatted for a minute or two, me standing on our little front porch and her a few feet away next to her bike. Just as we were saying goodbye, Cory joined us from inside the house, but before I could introduce him to my new acquaintance, he said a quick, surprised hello to her, she did the same, and then she rode away.

It was obvious they had met previously, and though Cory is the most emotionally composed person I've ever met, I like to think of myself as keenly discerning. There was tension in the air. Dying to fill in the gaps, I verbally lunged at him the second she was out of view.

"Do you know her?"

His response was a succession of short, bitten words. "Uh, yeah. She used to come into the congressional office all the time. We didn't see eye to eye."

Basically, a few years prior, when Cory worked as the district director for our local congressman, a staunchly conservative Republican, Claudia, a liberal-leaning Democrat, had made some visits to the office. Each time, the two of them had ended up gridlocked about whatever topic had brought her in. Though they avoided personal attacks, I'm guessing they pegged each other as stubborn, rigid, misguided, maybe even ignorant or naïve. As strangers, they were afforded the comfort of clinging to their long-held loyalties with no concern for how they might be felt from a different angle. It's impossible to engage in healthy, productive listening while simultaneously building a competing argument. It's safe to assume Cory hadn't been trying to learn from her, and he certainly didn't try to connect with her in a meaningful way.

I suddenly worried we had set up in enemy camp. How many others were there in this neighborhood?

In the past we had lived in communities where most everyone had held virtually the same opinions and views. Listening isn't hard in an echo chamber. It's all just reverb. Music to the ears. But here, in a city and life ripe with clashing contexts, histories, beliefs, and opinions, I was forced to realize what an actual wreck I am at listening. There's no coasting through conversation anymore, a prospect that thrills me. Yet I am often more concerned with what I'm about to say than I am with what was just said to me. More often than I'd like to admit, I'm more interested in the sound of my own voice.

How does this happen? If we take a step back and evaluate the world we live in, we'll realize that we are deeply imbedded in a culture that constantly lunges for the mic. We value making our voices heard and getting our points across. But if our goal is healthy community and loving our neighbors, we need to rethink our approach. Before we can learn from each other, before we can truly grow into a clearer picture of God's good kingdom, we have to fall in love with listening.

God created our five senses as a way for us to understand our world—and Jesus referred to them often—but, as it turns out, talking is not one of them. Only as we engage in the hidden practice of listening do we learn about the struggles of others, gaining empathy where we once cast judgment.

Jesus admonished us to "pay close attention to what you hear. The closer you listen, the more understanding you will be given" (Mark 4:24). I was rocked by the simple clarity of his words. There's no room for interpretation here. He warned us to listen closely to his voice while actively demonstrating a life of attentively listening to those around him. This is the heart of relationship, though it grows more old-fashioned with every passing digitized day.

Once I realized how much work I had to do, I became serious about not only *how* I was listening, but *who* I was listening to. I intentionally forged relationships with those I wanted to learn from, and I tried my best to listen more than I spoke (though it's possible my early successes were few). I sought those outside my viewpoints on social media. I read different books—listening with my eyes.

Along the same lines, Cory and I attended the Justice Conference, a gathering of people who share a concern for the vulnerable and oppressed. Sitting far from the glare of the spotlight, I jotted pages of notes, cramming thoughts into the margins, nearly draining my pen. For two days we listened to people of color talk about their experiences in the church and the broader world. For hours on end, our hearts were scorched with the burn of their truth.

It was uncomfortable. Energizing. They begged us to join our voices with theirs, but before that would even be possible, before we could speak without unintentionally inflicting damage, we had to commit to listening. That meant not just hearing their words, but focusing with our entire beings, attending to what they were saying, heart and soul. Careful, mindful listening was the only possible starting point for a much-needed jolt to our worldview.

Perhaps ironically, the evening we returned home, Silas plucked a question seemingly from the summertime clouds floating over us: "Mom, are you white?"

I bristled, my brain thrusting into overdrive, imagining where this question might lead and quick to deflect any potential discomfort. "Uh, yeah. My skin would be called white," I stammered.

He studied his arm, already deepening its shade from the

short two weeks of June under our belts. "Can I be called whitish? It would be easier to be white."

From across the patio, Calvin chimed in, "Yeah, it would be."

My oil-and-water, Korean-born sons had landed on a rare point of understanding over what they saw as a shared misfortune, one they knew they would never be able to change.

Here's what I wanted to do. I wanted to remind them again how beautiful their skin is. I wanted to tell them how I wish mine wasn't so pale. I wanted to offer easy, churchy platitudes about God's perfect design. I wanted to hush them, to tell them to go run around and get sweaty. I wanted to shut down the intensity of their human experience by filling it with my own wiser words. What mother wouldn't race to cover the tender wounds of personal identity and belonging with the quick-sticking Band-Aids of "I love you" and "God made you exactly as he did for a reason"?

I wanted to be the one with the answers. And, though I may not have realized it at the time, I wanted them to begin to distrust their feelings and discount their experiences, to shush them back beneath the surface—all in the name of my comfort, to minimize my own fears and to pretend for a moment that I could spare them their own. Instead, I remembered the men, women, and children from the conference we had just returned from, and I listened. I passed them the mic, so to speak, and didn't reach for it until they were finished. I had no simple words of encouragement, no quick fixes, and didn't pretend otherwise.

I walked away with a better understanding of who they are and what they face, even within a community known for its inclusivity and heart. I was surer than ever that I would do whatever it took to help create a more peaceful world for my beloved sons and daughter and for all who are dragged down by the weight of their difference. But this clarity would not have arrived if I had prioritized my own voice over theirs.

We change, soften, sharpen, and grow as we gather with and listen to those who are not replicas of ourselves and whose experiences are outside of our own. I learn this lesson again and again. So far, I have not outgrown my need for reminders.

And yet, when I am reminded, I see there are so many ways to build this practice into everyday life, no wrong way, really. First, we have to reimagine ourselves as students of the invisible practice of mindful hearing. We have to reacquaint ourselves with quiet and minimize distraction so that our ears can be tuned. Here's how I try. I make space each day to intentionally choose silence, going about my business without the drone of music, podcasts, or television. I also leave my phone at home whenever possible, particularly on walks. It seems like such an unremarkable choice, we're tempted to dismiss it. There are times I suffer a wave of lowest-grade panic that I'll miss out on capturing a beautiful moment without a camera in my pocket. Yet what I lose in my ability to document the visible I gain in the audible, that vibrant world that blends so seamlessly into the physical, waiting to be heard. There, in the quiet, my place comes alive. It's priceless.

Right now, I could rattle off my zip code or even pass

along the GPS coordinates of our home, but it wouldn't tell you much. Or, I could share the playlist of our summers. There's the tinny, anemic music piped from the ice cream truck that creeps down my street several times a day. From my living room windows I hear businesswomen and men talking shop on one of their routine walking meetings. There's the whir of bike tires, the squeak of stroller wheels across the sidewalk, a consoling cadence of motherhood leaking out from the edges of a language I don't understand. Thumping rap and peeling mariachi horns punctuate the white noise of tires on asphalt, and, if you're listening closely, you'll hear the great whoosh of water dropping from the bucket at the splash pad and onto a squealing pack of suntanned kids. A train whistle blares almost continuously, the audible reminder of who we are and why we're grateful all the same. Big rigs barrel north a street away as scooters and mopeds defy the dehumanizing efforts of a justice system run amuck, loyally delivering pushed-out neighbors to factory jobs across town. All the while, cicadas pray at my feet and songbirds teach me to worship.

Written into the melody of everyday life, I nod along with Sara Miles, who wrote, "For me, paradise is a garden, but heaven is a city."[1] Can you hear us?

As we hone this skill of tuning in to the world we're in, we're better positioned to really begin to hear the people near us.

I happen to be stirred into a true melting pot, each of us falling wildly off the map of who the others always thought we were. Single moms, tattooed men, refugees and immigrants, activist liberals, dyed-in-the-wool conservatives, addicts, business owners, and undocumented college students on the move. Some are orphans and some might wish they were. Each reveals the face of God, made in his image in order to bounce his glory and goodness around the room and through the streets.

I know not all areas are this eclectic. For the first twenty years of my life, I lived in a sweet community of people who appeared to align in most ways. But what I know now—and what my parents and those wiser than me knew all along—is that diversity finds its home in every quiet corner. Unearthing it might require a bit more sleuthing, but there is always someone near who has lived from a different vantage point, and she is the one we'll learn from most. Her presence stretches our long-held ideas about what really matters, forcing us to mine the depths of our discomfort as we dig in to who she is and why our lives have crossed.

Over the past two days, my Benjamin Moore White Dove walls have heard more f-bombs than in the preceding four years combined. There was a time I would have covered my ears, shamed it, and shooed it away. Now, I'm learning that this is the language of pain, the lyric of oppression. Bearing the burden of a wounded brother means letting heavy words fall lightly in my heart and, sometimes, even in my home.

Over the same two days I also heard a screaming match between two of my kids and recognized it as an invitation to diffuse their angst with truth. I listened closely as a friend shared with me about a new job opportunity and the anxieties of jumping the tracks into a future she hadn't planned. I listened as a woman recently released from jail offered the children's sermon on Sunday. "Devote yourselves to prayer with an alert mind and a thankful heart" (Col. 4:2), she shared. Paul's words, spoken through this unassuming missionary, are still moving through me like a straight-line wind.

Eugene Peterson wrote of our need to listen and wait, attend and adore. We unite as we listen, yielding the floor to another. We pay attention, fully present, when our lips aren't moving and our minds are alert. I am stunned by the richness of discussion this posture invites. I'm swept away by the freedom found in viewing people not as teammates or rivals but rather as friends and brothers.

Five years after running into Claudia that first time, I now consider her a friend. Cory does as well. Over cups of coffee, the two of them got to know each other as neighbors, rather than political opponents. I can't speak for her, but as time goes on and our dialogue spans years, we are learning from her. She is graciously, with tremendous kindness and thoughtfulness, leading us to see from a new perspective. Last year she won my enthusiastic vote in her bid in a local election. As a newly elected official, when she ran into a situation that pertained to incarceration rights, she enlisted Cory's help, and the two of them worked together for the good of our community. We've traded book recommendations and Netflix show reviews. We grabbed dinner one night with her and her husband and stayed out too late because there was just so much ground to cover.

"Listening is a form of spiritual hospitality by which you invite strangers to become friends," wrote Henri Nouwen.[2] Rather than spending all our time with those whose lives mirror ours so closely that all conversation distills into small talk, we are invited to widen our circle and hush our mouths. Do we dare imagine the possibilities? What if one year from now, you were part of a book club where you were the youngest in attendance, by decades? What if you found your way into a group of women who differ from you socioeconomically, on either end of the spectrum, resisting the urge to believe you don't belong among them and instead nurturing a surprising, genuine friendship? What if you showed up at a church across town pastored by a man or woman of color, then dutifully stuck around?

I recently came upon Silas belting out a song with confidence that belied the actual performance. "Joyful, joyful, we of Dorothy, God of Florida, Lord above!" For the rest of my days, I won't be able to hear that song without grinning. We will continue to get things wrong, reality warping against our unique experiences, our vision for the future, and the decibel level of our lives at any given moment. Listening well doesn't come naturally to any of us. It takes work, and most of our slips along the way will be nowhere as adorable as his.

But we aren't too old and rusty to learn something new, and it's never too late.

Open your windows. Turn off your phone. Walk the back alleys of your neighborhood. You live in the country? The suburbs? It might require a drive up the road, that's all. Go wherever life thrums and pops, the place common sense most loudly warns you to avoid.

Go *there*. Sit down. Lean in. Resist the urge to posture or interject. Listen without an agenda. Just wait and see where it takes you.

Chapter Four

Salted Chocolate

When we adopted our kids, we understood there was loss somewhere in the mix. This is the first-grade math of adoption. No matter the age of the child, no matter the circumstances surrounding the adoption, no matter whether it's open, closed, or somewhere in the middle, roots have been pulled, and the process of transplanting a heart is bound to be delicate regardless of the soil. We knew to expect some sadness and complicated feelings along the way. We anticipated some rocks on the path toward our togetherness. What we didn't fully grasp was that adoption—our road to parenthood—would be a portal to understanding suffering. Choosing to walk straight into the white-hot pain of our grieving kids was an important entry point to the discovery that some of the best gifts are laced with the deepest sadness.

For Cory and me, our faith, or at least our religion, had not equipped us to abide through dark days. I was taught victory was the fruit of belief. Suffering was a curse, always proof of something, and never good. The pastors I knew said their faith could fix the middle-class kid who robbed the convenience store or the druggie with red-rimmed eyes. It could quench red-hot lust and pull the devil out of a teenager like long strands of ribbon from a Black Sabbath cassette tape. We had been taught to avoid sorrow, to cast it out and pray it away, no easy task when the earth seemed to spin on an axis of hardship. But I came to see that I didn't want a faith that could move mountains. I wanted a faith that could ride out a howling stretch of pain, keeping its spark through the low winds of drought.

Years later, the church laid a wary eye on me and my uterus, empty as a secret. They offered special prayer services and pleaded with me to claim my healing, as though I was dying or in some way broken. But somehow, I knew grace when I saw it. "You don't know what your family picture hanging on the walls of heaven looks like, but it's beautiful," my mom told me. The possibilities, still hazy, began to fill with color. Over the next six years, I was handed three babies, nothing between us but a promise. No history, no DNA, no sweet gestation where they learned to be soothed by my voice. They came with the sort of loss that fades in intensity but hides somewhere within their growing frames. Some nights, their eyes get that faraway look and they cash in my permission to stare straight through me to all the "might have beens" for as long as it takes, knowing I'll be right there when they return.

Their arrival was an invitation to taste the bitter along with the sweet, to swallow it down and let it catch in our throats, a gift that taught us not to wish for the lie of easy comforts.

Between the exhaustion, self-doubt, and celebration of those early years; between potty-training, sticker charts, soft blankies warm from the dryer, birth families, peanut butter toast, slow healing, and pleading prayer, I was developing a taste for complexity.

In the book of John, as through all the Gospels and the entire New Testament, Jesus promised the opposite of what the world offers like a prized show pony. He held up things like smallness, humility, suffering, poverty, and the guarantee of outsider status, as though they were his best offerings. He knew what was at stake. He'd seen our wrong desires played out at eye level, yet he persisted. His life on earth was a decades-long exercise in rescuing us from the things we think we want by giving a face to the heart of God. "My purpose is to give them a rich and satisfying life" (John 10:10), he said. His central tenets of belief never changed: love the people around you, be relentless in the pursuit of holiness, and, oh, it'll cost you.

Say what?

Here's what's hard to understand about us humans: Jesus couldn't have made himself clearer about the inevitability of hardship, yet we are shocked when his promise rings true. When one of the gifts I'm handed looks like sadness, a lost opportunity, or something much worse, like suffering, I usually feel ripped off. I keep trying to barter my perceived obedience for the sweet life. Isn't this what I deserve? Isn't abundance best measured by the roses that grow, not the rain that grew them?

Jesus was a "man of sorrows, acquainted with deepest

grief" (Isa. 53:3), yet Western Christians, on the whole, remain emotionally allergic to sadness and discomfort. We do anything we can to avoid it.

Of course, we don't want to borrow trouble. I'm profoundly grateful for the grace of easy relationships and low-key days. It's not about craving pain or heaving around an outsized martyr complex. I don't want to imagine a world where that is the goal. We were made for contentment and celebration, yes. But that's not all.

The health and well-being of our communities depend on our willingness to taste sadness with joy and pain along with redemption. If we hesitate, hanging back when grief strikes or fearing the wobbly state of our neighbors' lives might threaten our peace, we have closed the door on peace itself. C. S. Lewis reminded us that God "whispers to us in our pleasures, speaks in our conscience, but shouts in our pain: it is his megaphone to rouse a deaf world."[1]

All throughout his time here on earth, Christ camped among the hurting. He didn't flee discomfort. He walked straight into it, then took off his shoes and stayed, accepting all of it as gift and nourishment. He offers the same abundance to us. We can hear it, as Lewis said, so very clearly when we're willing to step into the pain.

It was almost dusk when Cory saw our friend Jason trudging up the sidewalk, his earbuds jammed into his ears as usual.

Pulling up to the curb, Cory swung open the passenger door and Jason hopped in. Young, lanky, and handsome with a wide, easy grin, I find him impossibly lovable.

Jason is one of the people we've learned to carry in our hearts when he disappears for long stretches of time, holding on to him in ways he isn't even aware of and praying him home. Absorbing from a young age the message that he wasn't worth much and struggling to keep up with his gang-banging brother, he exists in the in-between of incarceration. For those with a record, there is no end to looking over their shoulders. Slipped beneath the microscope of our criminal justice system, it is a sobering reality that nothing more than a minor technicality or mistake wields the power to land them back on the wrong side of the razor wire. Like so many others we know, he rockets wildly between the hope of change and the plague of self-defeat.

The jail seems to have a strange, magnetic pull on him, the same force field that draws him back to its walls seems to repel him away from any steady job that comes his way. The plot-points rarely vary, but this is his story, every bit as important to him as the threads of my life are to me. The short drive was all the time Jason needed to fill Cory in on the basics.

"I'm making money." He chuckled, staring out the passenger window with lost eyes. "But I'm not working."

Twelve days later, Jason called, asking for a ride across town. This time he was strung out and suicidal. Any hope he'd fought to hold was now circling the drain. I was already in bed when Cory came home and filled me in. Those were the nights when sleep felt most like the enemy. I tossed and turned, pounding my pillow, imagining his apartment just half a mile away. *Is he there? Is his mom with him? Does she know he's hurting? Does she care?* For all the comfort close proximity can bring, when you find yourself fully sunken into the low terrain of no-matter-what love for someone clinging to the far edge of wellness, on the worst nights, their despair can feel like the half-life of your own. We stare at the ceiling while our calls are ignored, and morning waits at the end of an impossibly long corridor.

In his novel *Ordinary Grace*, William Kent Krueger wrote, "The miracle is this: that you will rise in the morning and be able to see again the startling beauty of the new day."[2] I suppose that's a more lyrical version of my heart's cry during those wide-awake nights. That's the miracle I want most for my neighbors, to be startled by the beauty of this world, and to see it as an expression of God's endless love for them.

Here in the land of the living, we are learning that no work on earth is ever finished. There's no clear moment of day or night, just minutes spent sliding away from the sun and then back again. There is no clean cut between bad and good, or lost and found. Most days, we're all a little of both, weary souls with failing night vision, just trying to make our way home.

When I was a kid growing up in the country, my dad taught me that the best way to carry something heavy is to carry something equally heavy in the other hand. From personal experience, this applies to buckets of water, overstuffed suitcases, concrete blocks, grocery bags filled with large cans of SpaghettiOs, and dense emotions.

Decades later, I remain a distracted and forgetful student of balance. Gratitude and sorrow aren't, as I once believed, mutually exclusive. They pair quite well together, one in each hand. It can be easy to ebb into the dark seas of sadness, staring too long at grief and disunity. The trick is to keep filling the other bucket. The sadness is real, but there is so much more to the story.

Today I lost a person I was never brave enough to love.

Today I'm a mom too tired for this tough parenting gig.

Today my friend sends tear-stained text messages, and I follow suit.

Today my child is sick, and no one can help him get better.

Today jail turned to prison.

But turn the page. Can you see it?

Here, our neighbors invite us over for their daughter's twelfth birthday party, heaping our bowls with spicy broth. The rest of them chatter rapidly in Spanish while we gesture wildly about the delicious food, our eyes and noses running from the *chiles*. After dinner, they bring out the cake, and after another moment of discussion we don't understand, they sing "Happy Birthday" in English, just so we can sing along.

Here, my addiction-afflicted soul sister shows up unexpectedly two nights in a row, bass bumping, to give me a hug and keep her word. I walk back inside to my family watching TV, the smoke from her cigarette clinging to my sweater, and I can't help myself. I call it all good.

Here, someone is hired. Someone falls in love. Someone celebrates seven months of sobriety, someone gets out of jail, so we bake a cake and plaster it with sprinkles.

The way of resurrection is also the way of the cross. It goes both ways. After a particularly gray season in our lives and neighborhood, a friend asked me with concern, "Are you still sad?" I responded truthfully. "Of course I am. I'm sad every day. I'm also happy every day."

Isaiah 25:8 speaks of God swallowing death forever and wiping away our tears. Only recently did I discover that some translations read, "The Lord God will wipe away the tears from all faces." A more obscure translation shows God wiping tears from "every cheek." After a lifetime of hearing, God will wipe the tears from every eye; this feels like an important discovery. We aren't supposed to live dry-eyed. No, we were made to feel pain. It rends us from ourselves. It smudges our view, hides us away.

Once we understand that pain is not an indictment on our faith, we're at liberty to feel sadness with our joy, a sprinkling of salt on bittersweet chocolate. There in its blending, we experience the solace of being stowed away in the shadow of God's wing along with everyone else.

Jesus promised us an abundant life, but abundance implies everything, both the sweet *and* the salty. All of it counts toward aligning our character to Christ's. This is real wealth, the startling opulence that leaves us fully satisfied. We won't find it in manufactured heartache or attached to the end of sin. It's not darkness we're after. It's real companionship, the kind that stares at the ceiling until morning breaks, no matter how long it takes.

Chapter Five

How to Love

Back when our house was being built, we were unprepared for the sheer amount of decisions that had to be made. Ours was a builder-grade home on a small, crooked lot. We were given very little wiggle room in terms of modifications or last-minute ideas. Still, there were the nitpicky details to contend with: countertops, cabinet hardware, and flooring options to name a few. When it came time to place light switches and outlets, we kicked our overthinking tendencies into high gear and delivered an electrical plan so detailed, so convoluted, so positively ridiculous, our builder thought we were kidding.

Five years later, we exist in a unique electronic purgatory crafted with our own ill-equipped minds, ruing the day we meddled with the process in the first place. Can we charge our phones on our nightstands? Not without an extension cord. Did we whimsically place a few outlets behind doors? Yes, we sure did. Do we have two outlets spaced less than a foot apart in our living room, neither of which is accessible from the couch? We'd rather not talk about it.

These weren't the only mistakes made. There were others along the way, though none as fortuitous as the three enormously oversized windows accidentally installed in our living room. To be sure, curtaining them is more involved than it was ever meant to be, yet I have found myself up to the challenge, sometimes even seasonally.

Over time, I have grown accustomed to seeing the entire world—or at least *my* entire world—through their gigantic, street-facing panes.

Every day, I quietly observe my neighborhood from the comfort of my gray couch, in the company of my multitudinous, irrelevant outlets. Our neighbor makes his succession of quick trips to town, returning with bags of fast food or a new pack of smokes. The sun filters through the spaces between the humble homes across the street on winter mornings, falling on unexpected details—the blue plastic baby swing tied to a sturdy limb, the stray cat dashing across three yards as if he owns this block and we exist for his entertainment.

I watch fat blue jays searching for seed. I see black squirrels with nut-packed cheeks. I see Bonnie setting out on her daily, two-mile walk. There's Linda. Stephanie. Brenna, with her pink-cheeked son tied to her chest. This is my place. This is home. It grows prettier to me by the day.

It should not come as a great surprise that, as I keep my eye on this spectacularly familiar place, the headlines warning about poverty, addiction, racism, chronic loneliness, and a culture set adrift by false intimacy become more than taglines and hot takes. They aren't just statistics. They aren't often even newsworthy. Now, what used to be two-dimensional words have grown arms and hands, forming my compass for caring. They point to actual lives of dynamic, complex people I know and love, men and women walking the sidewalks with me in pursuit of the same things—to exist with meaning, to belong, to wring every drop of hope from the world we're in.

The thing about paying attention is that there's no ending point. Patterns emerge, low limbs of trouble stretching wide across our world, dropping rotten fruit into our own backyards. There is nothing new under the sun. Nor is there anything hypothetical. The problems we once saw swirling in the atmosphere hover closer to home than we would have imagined. And at the point we understand this truth, we have a choice to make.

Last fall I noticed a young boy trudging down the street toward the park in his bright blue coat, hood up, head down. Mack was twelve years old, and he should have been in school.

Months earlier, he and his brother had spotted me pulling into my driveway from across the street. The younger brother had yelled my name, "Ms. Martin! Ms. Martin! Hey, Calvin's mom!" They ran toward me, offering to help unload the van. They wanted a job, any job. Like all of us, they wanted to be needed. I loaded them each down with a cardboard box and led them down to the basement, where they carefully lined them up against the wall.

Now, here he was again, walking by my window in the middle of the school day. The neighborhood rumor mill, fueled primarily by dramatic middle-school boys, had been in overdrive with news about recent trouble at the bus stop.

Several of our fine, young citizens had been suspended. I had heard the gossip, but they should have all been back in school by now. Why was one of them still outside milling around? I started keeping an eye out for Mack every day around two o'clock. He would shuffle to the park, staring at his feet. Sometimes he sat in a swing like he would a chair, stock still. Sometimes he kicked at an invisible opponent, or maybe just the dirt. Other times, he meandered aimlessly, past the park, past the chain-link fence covered in vines, and straight out of my line of vision.

Eventually, I gathered the nerve to get nosy, conveniently planting myself in his path. I'm a woman, after all. I know how to engineer being at the right place at the right time. And so it was.

It turned out Mack had been expelled from school, but the details were hazy. I was concerned for him, bent on gathering the pieces of the puzzle that had been lost along the way. Though I wasn't sure there was anything to be done, what mattered more was that Mack and his family quite abruptly mattered to me. After that, it became virtually impossible to concentrate on anything other than watching out my window for him each day.

Mack's mom began stopping by my house to chat some nights on her walk home from work. Tears dripped from her chin to my fake wood floors as she parceled out fresh chapters from the story of their lives. The highlights: She loved her family fiercely. She worried about them constantly. She felt overwhelmed by the pressure to guarantee their total perfection.

She wanted someone to believe in them, in her, in her ability to parent them well despite limited resources. Over time, a friendship formed between us. We had each other's backs.

Along the way, I began to love Mack and his family, their radiant charm and easy laughter winning me over without a fight. We were starting to belong to each other, and once that happens, all bets are off. "To love your neighbor is never safe. But it is always good," said Pastor Gabriel Salgueros, president of the National Latino Evangelical Coalition.[1]

One evening, I was about to head out for a PTO meeting when I heard a ruckus outside. It was typical sibling malcontent, except it lasted well beyond the acceptable limit of garden-variety brother drama. I opened the door, and there they were, Mack and his two youngest brothers. One was sobbing, one was fuming, and the third was caught in a maelstrom of both.

The nuances of their feud clearly outpaced the scope of my understanding, and I had neither the time nor the desire to play referee. I wasn't feeling good-neighbor vibes at that particular juncture. I was in full-on mom mode, in a hurry and emotionally unmoved. Fine, I was annoyed. Still, I found myself startlingly invested in *them*, agenda be danged. Staring into their faces lined up just inside my front door, some shiny with tears, I launched into the abbreviated version of my classic mom lecture.

"One day, you will be best friends. If you get married, he will be the one standing next to you. If you find yourself in a heap of trouble, he will be the one you call." Then, just in case

I hadn't already blurred the boundaries enough, I went down the line one by one, cupped their faces in my hands, and told them I loved them by name. I don't know what came over me.

The boys were stone-cold silent. There were no tearful apologies. They didn't return my affections. In their eyes I saw flashes of profound alarm, a desire to run away quickly, and a seriousness that assured me they were receiving the weirdness I was dealing.

I tossed them each a granola bar and told them to go play.

Our relationship had only begun. I didn't yet see the full scope of complication looming on the horizon for Mack, or the ways his presence would breathe life into my days. I didn't yet know that his justice would be tied, in part, to my surrender. With every hello and each box of granola bars, I was learning that loving my neighbors, awkward as it can be, did not have to be treated as nuclear fusion, reserved only for the cerebral and highly trained. It was much simpler than I imagined. And infinitely sweeter.

In our heads, we understand that everything we accomplish is pointless if we cannot be known as people who love freely and fully. In our hearts, we long to be reminded of our secure place at the center of God's beating heart. Love is compelling. It's comforting. We are driven by our deep need for it. We've known the fulfillment of passing it around. It's in and around us, the great prize of life, if you boil it all down. But it sure doesn't seem simple a lot of the time. Or, at least, we don't want it to be.

So often, we get busy trying to make its scale match its

significance. If it's as big a deal as Jesus said it is, then we need to be sure we don't mess it up. We need to study love, stew on it, pick it apart, and fashion it into something worthy of the title. We endure untold sermons and Bible studies on what it might look like to truly love our neighbor. We read books and blogs, discussing them with our friends, but we never seem to take the actual step of getting outside of our churches and homes to do something about it. Putting wheels on our head knowledge and skating out into the world with our hearts exposed sounds terrifying, and the stakes feel too high.

We want to do better. We simply can't help it. The urge is pressed into our souls like the thumbprint of God, a primal longing of which sin attempts to rob us. But the question is how? How exactly are we supposed to give legs to this inborn desire to become a community of compassion, kinship, and love? Where do we start?

What I'm learning is that it's as simple as looking out the window and noticing. As we go looking for magnificence in the ordinary corners of the world, hard lines will blur. Fences will fall. As our love for our place deepens, our love for its people will flourish. Just as the boys ran to help me carry in crates of peonies, we will find ourselves breaking from the conventional wisdom that says we are to mind our own business. Maintaining a safe distance asks nothing of us. It's so easy to tip into judgment when we view the world through an us-them dichotomy. Sitting face-to-face, the problems loom larger and we have to contend with the sticky fact that there is simply always more to the story. Looking at our neighbor with compassion rather than scorn, we'll soon discover why Jesus made such a fuss about it. Father Boyle wrote, "We have a chance, sometimes, to create a new jurisdiction, a place of astonishing mutuality, whenever we close both eyes of judgment and open the other eye to pay attention. . . . Suddenly, we find ourselves in the same room with each other and the walls are gone."[2]

We want to love.

We want to be loved.

Being part of a loyal community that looks out for one another is far more than a pipe dream. It's a privilege. It's a promise. Standing together, we're safer. We're stronger. We're more aware of our own frailty and less prone to navel-gazing. Living entangled is such an obvious win.

A few months ago our friend Damon sat at our kitchen island, stirring a cup of hot tea. He and Cory became friends over at the jail, and now Damon was on the cusp of actual freedom. There's a unique wisdom earned by the careful reflection that comes on the heels of rock bottom, a humble clarity. To say I pay close attention to this wisdom would be an understatement. My job in these situations is to brew strong tea and lean in.

As was usually the case, Damon held no illusions about how he had landed in the system. Similarly, he showed no hubris about his personal abilities to keep it from happening again. But he was hopeful, and he had given it a lot of thought. His plan involved a healthy version of community, where each of us actively brings our experiences to the table, along with our successes and failures. Rather than being chained to our own limitations, we learn from each other. Aren't we all just out here, gathering clues, trying our best to hit the mark on love and belonging?

"I think we can learn something every minute of every day." Damon paused, a burly, good-hearted man sipping Lady Grey tea from a flowered vintage mug. "We just have to pay attention."

This is the Word of God whispered for me and you, from the lips of my war-weary neighbor. This is how we love, by focusing so intently on each other that we can't help ourselves. We watch from our windows. We venture outside. We receive the help that's offered. We find ourselves connected in spite of everything we once thought stood between us.

You carry my boxes. I pass out granola bars and impromptu affections.

Wedged between these seemingly trivial moments, we remember our hearts of flesh coated with the fingerprints of love and simply throw up our hands in surrender.

We stop resisting our spiritual DNA, which bends us hard toward the way of mercy.

We taste the possibility and power of ordinary, luminous love, and discover we can't get enough.

Part Two

Love Like a Neighbor

Chapter Six

Misfits, Randoms, and Regulars

For the first three and a half decades of my life, I wondered why God created Mondays. I have lived its every cliché: spacing appointments, locking myself out of the house, getting stuck outside in a rogue rainstorm. Years ago my birthday fell on a Monday, and the universe gifted me a speeding ticket on my morning commute.

Songs have been written about Mondays' bad vibes, and I have been right there on the risers with the rest of humanity, singing along in my low alto.

Seven years ago, though, my Mondays were reborn. It began entirely by chance, as most good things do. Three couples, none of us particularly close at the time, decided to meet together as we each navigated a similarly jarring juncture in our faith. Desperate for a soft place to process the change heaving toward us, we recognized an ache in our souls that could only be relieved by the close compression of other men and women also rerouting from the futures they had imagined.

It felt both late in life and much too early to ask open-ended questions about what it really meant to follow Christ. Each of us was discovering how unwelcoming the church could be for those deemed skeptical or even overly curious. So, we drew together on the loneliest day of the week at six o'clock sharp. By eight, we were fortified. Comforted. Galvanized that, though the path before us was a twisting thing, it mattered. And we were not left walking it alone.

The group grew and evolved over time. Our original crew of three families expanded. Not long after our family moved, we knew that we could either continue reaching back for what was comfortable or move toward the lumbering vulnerability of cobbling together a similar group in our brand-new city. We couldn't do both. We had to choose: the comfort of the past or the struggle of moving forward.

I wish I could tell you it was clean and simple, that we jotted down a guest list of families in our target demographics, ensuring that our life stages, kids' ages, and dietary and theological preferences all fell into alignment, then *poof!* they all showed up and it was bliss.

I wish I could impress and inspire you with a four-step plan for starting a vibrant neighborhood Bible study built to last.

Either option would be more appealing than the truth, which is that we hemmed and hawed for almost two years before our clawing hunger for friendship sprung us into ill-planned action. We sent out a handful of text messages based on the simplest criteria: (1) Did they live in our city? and (2) Did they, like us, seem to carry a shadow of loneliness, a tinge of spiritual discomfort, or both?

A few joined us, and the Misfits were born. For the first four months our fledgling group met in our unfinished basement on couches from the 1980s. We bundled up that winter in granny-square afghans and tucked our feet under ourselves, as far away from the frigid concrete floor as possible. Fenced in by cardboard boxes of junk we didn't need and within eyeshot of our makeshift pantry—jars of green beans and applesauce lining a Sam's Club plastic folding table—we got to work getting to know one another. Every Monday night spent balancing Styrofoam bowls of gluten-free macaroni and cheese on our knees took us one layer deeper into the stories that shaped us.

I am sure there are few honors as significant as being invited by a near-stranger into a slow-growing place of mutual trust. Still, we were far from ideal. There were nights the babysitter flaked and we couldn't eke out two verses of John down in our frigid bunker before a preschooler infiltrated with requests for a second brownie. We had several people show up once and then never return. There were times I wished in my truest heart that every single person would call in sick and we could pretend, at least for a week, that none of this had ever happened.

They don't call it "building" community for nothing. It is positively taxing work, the sort of grind that demands to be seen as necessary, at times detached from our particular feelings. Ours is not a story of a cute, color-coordinated collection of hipsters "doing life" with one another. Instead, we ebbed and flowed and took the summer off. We moved to the fellowship hall of our church, where a former jail inmate showed up and insisted we begin studying Hebrews, a book not exactly famous for its pith and whimsy, then left us there, never to return.

We moved down to the church basement, having been displaced by two merging Girl Scout troops, then up to the coffee room, then way up to an abandoned youth group room that hadn't seen activity in years, and back down again. Flexibility and faithfulness are basic requirements for the flourishing of any community.

Along every leg of our journey, the group dynamics shifted and fused. Neighbors began dropping in, and often back out again. Without meaning to, we became a place of refuge for stragglers and strugglers alike, who somehow knew their kind when they saw it. People shrouded in depression and others strung taut with anxiety sat silent for weeks on end, having grown accustomed to their voices being regarded as unwelcomed at the table. Then, when they understood that they were as vitally important as everyone else in the room, we had to settle on an underground protocol for redirecting conversation, so that everyone had time to share.

Last Monday evening I sat with our skeleton crew, the ten of us most likely to show up on any given week. After sharing the customary pitch-in meal that is usually as eclectic as the group itself, the kids ran off to play and us adults huddled up in Matthew, where we had been camped out for the past eighteen months because we were equal parts committed and meandering in conversation.

There was no flowery prayer, no singing, no trendy Bible study streaming from a smart TV. There were no bells and whistles, no shiny incentives.

There was the breath of God splayed open, a meal in itself, and our hearts a patchwork of mixed metals, welded through the communion of fried chicken and store-bought cookies. Two couples, six singles. Immigrants and formerly incarcerated. Republican and Democrat. Rich and poor. Culinary wizards and "I'll bring the spoons." KJV and NLT. Married, divorced, kids, no kids, Methodists, Mennonites, and blissfully unaffiliated.

This is us.

We don't *do* life together as much as we redefine it as a collective, one body in need of all its parts. This is our new, weekly rhythm. We remind each other and ourselves that we were called to discomfort, and that sometimes discomfort looks like a new friend short on social graces. We have so much to learn from each other. As Becca recently intoned, "This will be the year of astonishing enlightenment." She was right, as usual.

Come on in. We are all painfully aware of the ways we don't quite fit, and we will always make room for you. You can't scare us off or offend us. We're quick to laugh and gracious in our disagreements—of which there are plenty. We bear a striking resemblance to many of the casseroles and strange stews that grace our Monday-night table—not so pretty to look at, but immensely satisfying, sometimes a little spicy, and warm enough to get us through both the long days ahead and the seventy-seventh straight week in the gospel of Matthew, where convicting, mystifying parables abound.

If I could require fieldwork for each of you (and I suppose I can, because, honestly, who is going to stop me?), it would be to find a way to regularly break bread with the most random, regular people you can find. They're everywhere, once you make a habit of searching. They might be the ones avoiding eye contact or sticking to the smallest shreds of small talk. They're the ones you might overlook, for no other reason than the fact that they have learned to stay quiet. They're working at the pizza place. They're staring at their phones in the pick-up line. You have no idea how badly your random, regular self needs them near.

You don't have to plan annual vacations together or go changing your will. With any luck at all, there will be some oversized personalities in the group and hopefully someone who grates on you just a little. This is precisely what keeps us tender.

Find the strangest crew you can. Pull them from the far corners of your reach and draw them in. Do you know someone who seems a little needy? Depressed? Hyper? Overly shy? Too opinionated? Extra cranky? Perfect. They're on the list. Have you noticed the mom who seems really nervous? Do you know how to reach the guy who had a recent brush with the law? Or the neighbor who seems overwhelmed by her kids? Or the cashier who always remembers you by name? On the list. I promise. I mean it.

Our tendency to group ourselves according to shared

demographics has caused us to miss the most important one: a longing to be known just as we are, in all our rumpled-jeans, misbehaving-kids, tired-eyes nonglory. And, at the end of the day, isn't that all of us?

Offering ourselves as a kind-hearted presence in a world that has forgotten the meaning of community is a courageous act of peace. Set a date. Make some calls. Bring a dish to share, your Bible, your nagging questions, and even your opinions.

This is the way of growth and renewal. This is where lasting change begins.

Chapter Seven

Whopper Extra-Value Meal

Yesterday was Mother's Day. Over the span of the twelve years that I have been a mother—in its traditional "these kids are in my care and I'm responsible for teaching them how to do everything from sign their names in cursive (so easy) to not chew with their mouths open (most impossible task in the Western world)" sense—my Mother's Days have run the gamut of tender and sweet to, "Wait. Today was Mother's Day?" As with most of life, yesterday fell somewhere in the middle.

I woke up relieved to hear the kids quietly watching a cartoon together, rather than making me breakfast in bed. It's not that I'm a terrible mom devoid of sentimental feelings; it's just that me and my molars are still recovering from choking down a plate of scrambled eggs mixed with uncooked rice last year.

"It's Asian fusion!" one of my proudly Asian children had said.

There wasn't anything special planned this year, and I was more than okay with that. No gifts, save the homemade silk corsage Ruby made for me at Girl Scouts. No cards. No breaks from our usual Sunday routine. It was simply the chance to remember how special our ordinary really is, to kiss my kids' faces, understanding poignantly just how much they sacrificed to make me a mama. We talked about their birth moms—how could we not?—but there were no tears this year as there sometimes are. There were schemes, daydreams, and a general air of satisfaction that this life we were handed, though not without its share of bumps, is exactly the life we needed.

As with every other Sunday, our day officially began with our walk to church. One of my favorite things about our church is the small gathering of smokers that congregates just outside the doors after service is dismissed. I can't imagine a better welcome sign for the neighborhood, or to myself. "Come, just as you are. We mean it."

As we were heading home after the service, one of the group nonchalantly handed me a card.

Lisa started out as a neighbor who wandered into a Sunday service with her husband Bobby. In a congregation that hovered around forty on a good Sunday, it's impossible for newcomers to slip in and out unnoticed. Ours is not the place for anonymity. But while I had always noticed visitors, I had never before chased people down as they tried to sneak out during the last hymn. Sometimes, our souls simply recognize our kin before the rest of us understands why. I found them in the coffee room, stirring powdered creamer into their foam coffee cups. I don't remember exactly what I said to them, and part of me is glad. Usually, like any good introvert, I avoid putting people on the spot. But there was something about them that had drawn me in from across the room. Something deep within me had panicked at the thought that they might disappear as easily as they had arrived. I knew they were stalk-worthy.

Bobby's arms were a landscape of rage, scrawls and sketches merging into a canvas of emotional retreat. Three gothic letters were inscribed across his throat. The ink was the same blue-black I have come to identify as the DIY sort that pumps through the veins of jails and prisons. I wondered if they were at the service because of Cory. It wasn't entirely uncommon for men to come looking for him "on the outs."

As it turned out, they were new to the neighborhood, living in a house just around the corner. They hadn't been invited by anyone and made no mention of Cory. After a decade of struggle and life on the run, they simply found themselves pulled toward the hope of the church. The next Sunday, when they defied all logic and returned to the scene of my coffee room accosting, I took it as a sign and raised the stakes, inviting them to dinner later that evening. This marked the first time I had ever invited strangers into my home, and at the time the thought of it made me jittery. An hour before they were set to arrive, if I could have clawed back in time and retracted the offer, hand to heart, I would have.

But if anyone bore a risk in this odd convergence, it wasn't me. I'm still surprised they showed up that first night, to the unfamiliar home turf of perfect strangers. When we dare to move toward, rather than away from, each other, our reward is the solace of intimacy. There, the burdens of life rest lighter against our shoulders. There, our cynicism is chipped away, replaced with wonder. The topography of our relationship with Bobby and Lisa has been marked with mountaintops and low terrain. It has not been without heartbreak, but, as we are learning, there in the blackest night, the moon shines brightest. Ask me to paint a portrait of courage and hope, and I'll do my best to render their faces. Now, three years from our first meeting, they are two of our closest friends.

Over the years, Lisa has waved me in to both her sadness and her joy, and I find myself at home in both. In sharing her world without filters or excuses, my own world tilts a bit nearer to the sun, just as God intended. I love her.

But a card on Mother's Day still caught me off guard.

I opened it quietly in my bedroom as soon as I got home, before the lunch rush and the revolving door that our Sundays have become. A restaurant gift card fell out, and my eyes welled up.

Later that night, after a full day of discount pizza, pick-up basketball, shade-tree sitting, and two dozen seemingly unheard reminders to my little cherubs that all I wanted for Mother's Day was for them to get along, I remembered Lisa's loopy blue handwriting and the words that had disarmed me. As far as tangible presents go, I had only received one that day, this one from my sister in the complexities of life, a woman who has known the two-sided coin of motherhood. Though material gifts aren't the currency of love or friendship, I know what her gift cost her. Playing it cool is not an option when it comes to accepting frivolous gratitude from people caught in hard places. It is one of the most humbling experiences of my life, guaranteed to bring my heart to its knees in two seconds flat. And it happens all the time.

———

I have long understood the American concept of neighbors. They are the ones who live next door. The ones we wave at, now and then. The ones we might gift with cookies during the holidays. They are the nice people who keep a comfortable distance. It's likely we might never learn their names. But maybe the American idea of neighbors doesn't match God's idea. He invites us to something deeper, calling us to join him in loving each other and promising it will be worth the vulnerability it's sure to cost us. He points us to the heart of the matter: aligning with our neighbors will change our lives if we let it. But before we can offer them anything, we first have to be mindful students in the uncomfortable art of receiving.

———

When my doorbell rang last August, Michelle was the last person I expected to be waiting on the other side. I'd only met her a few times in the four years we had lived on the same street, and none of those times had been particularly noteworthy. I made an effort in the beginning, dropping cookies off at Christmas and greeting her by name when she visited our church a couple of times. Though friendly, she kept her distance. (This, too, is part of neighboring, recognizing everyone has different boundaries and doing our best not to force our own upon the guarded or resigned.)

It was only a week into a new school year, and the August air outside hung in damp sheets. Breathe in, breathe out; it felt more like swimming. Rivulets of sweat coursed down her temples. In a profound act of God's goodness, I remembered her name.

"I'm so sorry to have to ask you this," she said, "but I don't have a phone right now and I just got this notice in the mail. They're going to shut off our electricity, but it's a mistake. Is there any way I could borrow your phone and call?"

I waved her in out of the heat and handed her my phone. I still remember the tension in the air as she laid bare all the things weighing her down to the customer service operator on the other end of the line while I tried to look busy. So often, I have gone to some lengths to sweep any minor life issues beneath the rug of my optimism, my work ethic, my has-it-all-togetherness. Being left with no choice but to listen in as a woman I barely knew begged to be heard and apologized for mistakes she hadn't even made was just another example of the pride that still separated me from the people I most wanted to love.

She handed my phone back, her discomfort as real as the ballad of the cicadas sailing the humidity. "You can use my phone anytime," I promised. "It's no trouble at all."

In the weeks that followed, I saw her most days. She was hard at work ironing the kinks from a series of misunder-standings that hovered with its finger over the switch. My friendship with Michelle grew as she was repeatedly left with no option but to ask for help, and I did everything in my power to flatten any division this dynamic might have built between us. I jumped at every chance to hang out with her, not because it made me feel useful, but because I enjoyed her company. She made my days better.

Our conversations never lasted long, but we began to inch past small talk, portioning out slivers of our personal lives and passing the fork. Each of us had a child starting middle school, so we shared the relief of stewing together. She loved her family. She was a little on the shy side. She longed for connection. She reminded me so much of myself.

One morning I picked her up to take her to an appointment, and she handed me an intricate, handmade necklace. In the center was a tree crafted from tiny green beads, the trunk a delicate twist of copper wire. Dangling from the lowest branch was one tiny black bead. A tire swing. "I made it for you. It reminds me of the cover of *Falling Free*."

Fall swept through. Eventually, though, as her life regained its footing again and the immediacy of the crisis passed, the length between our visits stretched.

I was putting groceries away one day when her name popped up on my phone. "I was wondering if you've had lunch yet, but I'm sure you have . . ." she said, her voice trailing off.

I told her I hadn't.

"I have a coupon for Burger King, and I thought maybe we could have lunch together?"

Listen, I am no fast-food snob. I consider a week special

if I end up in the Taco Bell drive-through, and if I manage to get there twice, well, the world is my oyster. But it had been a very long time since I'd been to Burger King. (I was still a little skittish and unmoored over their ill-advised invention of Chicken Fries.) I put the rest of the groceries away, my mind in overdrive. *What on earth will I order? What was the best way for me to position myself at the register as payer?*

My heart held nothing but kindness, but my mistake, as usual, was the assumption that she needed my help. I should have known better.

When we got to Burger King, I made sure to be the first in line and reached for my wallet after we ordered two Whopper Extra-Value Meals for ten dollars, as the coupon offered. "Oh, no," she said. "This one is on me."

For the next hour, the two of us sat in a booth under fluorescent lighting, cable news screaming at us from the television bolted to the wall. Our political views didn't match any more than our life experiences did, but we were still two moms with fountain Cokes, worrying about our kiddos and dreaming our own dreams. I lined up tiny paper cups of ketchup on my plastic tray and dunked those fries with gusto. I ate every single bite of my Whopper-with-everything-no-cheese. I swallowed down the truth for the umpteenth time that the path from neighbor to friend only feels long when we watch each other from a safe distance. When we share our actual lives, swinging open the door to the details that define us—our preferences, our favorites, our fears—the atmosphere draws closer, and the world feels smaller and far less lonely.

As we walked back out to the van, I thanked her for my lunch.

"I'm glad we did this," she said. "I've been saving that ten-dollar bill for a special occasion, and when the coupon came, I knew I'd found it."

We parents do our best to teach our kids that it's better to give than receive, but we hide a secret behind our backs—not only is giving better, it's often easier. We're conditioned to repay kindness almost reflexively, quick to balance the ledger, preferably with interest. But when generosity is tossed back like a hot potato, can we really call it generous? Oh, how we hate our own poverty. Yet the benevolence of Christ leans toward kinship, where we take turns being filled with the feasts of wanting and relief. Here, we begin to identify with the king who came to save us through the thin chatter of a child, all naked need and wide-eyed expectation, palms open, no status to be shaken.

Without the weariness there is no thrill of hope. Without receiving, we miss the richness of giving. Without accepting what we do not deserve, we miss Emmanuel in our living rooms and all around town.

Not long ago, I wrote a column in my local newspaper about the pleasure of vibrant community, and a crotchety man repeatedly taunted me from the comments: "I pity your neighbors! Everyone just wants to be left alone!" Here's how much of his sass I'm buying: none of it. It might be true in isolation, but as a whole, we're pretty desperate to belong and be included. We don't have to be attached at the hip, strong-arming our way into each other's lives and hanging on like a shadow. We just need to reacquaint ourselves to the idea that we were created to *like* each other. Most of us want the kind of friendship that is defined by mutuality, where we're too busy enjoying each other to watch for pecking orders or power rankings. We don't need more colleagues or service providers. We want two-way streets paved with the truth that life is more bearable when we walk in the same direction.

Time after time, friends like Michelle and Lisa challenge my quiet assumption that there exists a slight tilt to the plane of our relationship, just enough for most of the giving to slide down to my end. Their big-hearted love keeps shaking the railings off my bad ideas about abundance, scarcity, and who deserves what.

In my efforts to untrain myself from these ideas, I started this list in my trusty spiral notebook awhile back:

Gifts from Our Neighbors

- Hand-me-down clothes
- Nike Air Jordan classics
- A quilt from Goodwill (Calvin's perennial favorite)
- A handmade bracelet
- A book of Egyptian mummy-shaped sticky notes for Silas
- A bottle of essential oils to treat Calvin's chronic mouth sores
- A cast-iron elephant bank

- A CD guaranteed to "wipe your hard drive if you ever need to"
- An airbrushed license plate adorned with the names of all my kids
- A vintage, ceramic glove form
- A bottle of "French" cologne

These are just some of the gifts we've received in the past year or so. In addition, there have been offers to babysit, loaves of pineapple bread, random boxes of cookies, and used books. Just one week ago, a friend shyly gave Cory a ring inscribed with the Lord's Prayer. "It seems like you're pretty into that God stuff," he muttered, staring at his feet. Without exception, these good gifts ripped my heart from my chest. In every case, loving my neighbor well has meant burying my pride and receiving immediately, without equivocation, and while wearing a smile. It's stone-cold impulse, and resistance is futile.

I now understand in a way that threatens my sense of order and entitlement what these gifts cost the giver. I also understand the paradox that material offerings of sincere love never cost as much as they pay. If I had to venture a guess, I'd say Cory will wear that ring until it disintegrates or his finger falls off, whichever comes first. This is who God is. This is how he loves us. Glad-hearted generosity is not reserved for the financially secure.

As surely as I sit here typing and crying at my dining room table, as sure as the wind blows every leaf sideways outside the window, as sure as the robins peck at the grass and the neighbor's sprinkler soaks the ground, as sure as the little boy across the street keeps growing—he's learned to ride a tricycle!—and as sure as his babysitter continues to speak to him with so much love in her eyes, her voice tilting up at the ends of her sentences, I have never done one single thing to deserve the piercing, sacrificial love of my neighbors. There are days I am sure I can't support its weight. I'd rather hold the hard stuff. I'm more comfortable lugging their burdens around than I am being doted on by them. I sort of hate bearing a debt.

These days, I'm learning that in the times I most desperately want my world to shrink down to a more manageable, personal size, the best thing I can do is walk into the thick of it with my arms outstretched, needy and unapologetic. Sometimes we open our door to give, but always we open our door to receive. We break the bread of human dignity and pass it around, baptizing our streets with the truth that each of us holds great worth. Here is the heart of generosity: gain resurrected from surrender. We receive its liberation with open hands and behold the illumination of our battered hope.

Chapter Eight

Tacos and Tea

About a year ago, a notable shift took place in our church congregation. Week by week, people from the neighborhood work release center (an incarceration facility where inmates are only allowed to leave for work and church) began filtering over, to our great delight. A few became a handful, and before long, they filled several rows. The men and women eventually filled in the side wings, and some of them began serving communion and passing the offering plate.

Because we're no strangers to the specific joys of friendship with those at the margins of society, this thrilled Cory and me. It also quickly changed the shape of our Sunday afternoons. Until that time, we'd considered Sunday a day of rest and a day set aside for family time. Now, we were faced with the reality that a growing number of the people in our lives were left with a short window of freedom each Sunday afternoon, but often no family to spend it with, no home to relax in, and usually no car to get them where they wanted or needed to go.

The solution was simple. The execution was, too, though

it would cost us some things, like down time and our Sunday afternoon naps.

With our home just two blocks from the church and only a few more blocks from work release, we put out an open invitation most Sundays. *Come.* The crowd varies a bit from week to week. There are a few regulars, who I put to work making coffee and chopping the occasional head of lettuce. They know where the sugar is and feel comfortable plopping down on the couch once their bellies are full. Some of them bring laundry, and they slip away to switch the load right around the time we're digging into dessert. Some visit loved ones stuck in jail via video chat, flipping their phones around so the rest of us can wave, say hi, and dream about the day they'll join us for hot soup or Hot-N-Ready pizza.

Other guests cycle in and out. On a blazing July afternoon, Jake was the new face at our table. He sat to my left out on the back patio table, his jeans two sizes too big, his glasses as thick as a double-paned window. Twice during the meal he stared down at his fidgeting hands, mumbling a quiet "thank you" for the meal. Glancing at the greasy paper plates with sloppy joes and chips straight from the bag, I hoped he understood that it really was no trouble. We sat for an hour under the shade of one small patio umbrella, six adults laughing and bumping elbows while the kids (some by age, others by virtue) raced around, trying to fabricate a zip line from trash found in our garage.

As usual, our conversation was all over the place. With the exception of our newest friend, the rest of us realized years ago that our bonds are real and built to last. Together at the table, nothing is off limits and everyone listens. With time and open-hearted patience, our Sunday crew is revealing a picture of what it truly looks like to come together regularly for the sake of the family.

Right now there's a lot of talk about what it might take to fix the problems plaguing our world. Legislation might help, our education system needs to be taken to school, and the church has its work cut out for it—the heaviest lifting waiting within its walls. Families are fractured, alienation abounds, and fear runs wild. Global conflict? Check. Rampant polarization? Check. Religious demonizing? Dinners with extended family where not even homemade mashed potatoes keep you from wanting to dash out the door? Yes. All are present and accounted for, looming overhead and casting long shadows.

But every Sunday I'm inclined to believe that making the world a better, brighter place might really be as simple as making lunchtime brighter for one person.

Most of us understand the importance of sitting around the table as often as possible with our families. While it's not always easy in practice, it's worth the time and effort. We know it's not about the food. My kids feel like the luckiest humans on planet Earth when we call cereal night and they each pour their own bowls.

We know it's not about the décor. If I called my family to a table with an elaborate tablescape, they would be baffled.

And we sure as heck know it's not about the condition of ourselves or our home. Once, when my kids were younger, I emerged after my shower wearing jeans rather than yoga pants, and Ruby started crying because she thought I was leaving for the night. (That's all you need to know about how I, a work-from-home mom with an aversion to getting ready, am seen in the eyes of the children. They take comfort in my no-fuss appearance and are as suspicious as cold-case detectives when the house is overly tidy.)

It begs the question: Why do we flip these truths when it comes to welcoming anyone else into our space? Why do we freak out? Why, oh why, do we keep forgetting that family is so much broader than the people who share our name and that we're all just looking for a genuine home?

Somewhere along the line, we have inferred that opening our home to someone is a special sort of gesture, and that the amount of work we put into that gesture indicates our degree of honor. We begin to believe our ordinary, or the way we actually live in the day to day, is not company worthy. We dig out the war paint, because we want our friends to feel honored and special. With gleaming intentions we veer into impressing. As it is said, we can compete or we can connect, but we can't do both.

The trickiest thing about writing about hospitality is that it requires using the word *hospitality*. I cringe. Heaven only knows why our desire to spend meaningful time with others is saddled with such a churchy, pearls-and-an-apron sounding word, conjuring up vivid Sunday school images of Mary and Martha. Even though I know Jesus preferred Mary's MO, I always feel like Martha was secretly the real winner of the contest. The fact that I still see it as a competition only further illustrates my need for this lesson in the first place.

Hospitality. It sounds kind of fancy, but its meaning is

simple, bare-bones, pure, and entirely holy—you are invited. There is room for you here, next to me. I receive you with gladness and offer my truest self. Here, we draw nearer to each other, seeking refuge from the crush of life. Here, we are safe. We are warm. We are free.

Knowing that, why does something so vital to our souls often feel scary and uncertain? What is it about the come-as-you-are spirit of hospitality that makes us doubt our ability to do just that? We can blame social media with its impulse to stage perfection and crop around the mess. We can point a finger at the individualistic bent of our modern age. I'm sure we all have a story or two to share about a time we put ourselves on the line in the name of welcome and walked away lonelier than ever. Rejection is a chronic injury, difficult to shake, once felt. We are so afraid our vulnerability won't be held with gentle hands.

The truth is, we still want more. Our ready skepticism wobbles on this one. Past disasters and potential future failures aside, we know it's worth it. We want to do better. We want to crack this nut. This inborn optimism to keep trying is all the proof we need: hospitality, the urge to gather, is hardwired into our spiritual and relational DNA. It might look a little different from person to person, but in this one way, we recognize our shared lineage of potlucks and patios, long nights where the wick burns down to an ember and the kids incite some small catastrophe. Despite all the mess and unpredictability, I'm positive it is worth taking some risks and making some mistakes to cultivate a consistent rhythm of welcome and belonging in our homes.

Speaking of mistakes, whoa, Nelly. Not only have I made my fair share, I *keep* making them while expecting a different result. For me, trouble comes knocking when I find myself overplanning, plotting, and scheming. It's usually when I start drafting make-ahead timelines and daydreaming about multiple courses and centerpieces that I careen straight into the pit of ruin.

Hear this clearly: there is nothing wrong with any of those things. My friend Sarah consistently invites me into her home, where garlic infuses the air and I can expect a table covered in vintage china, fresh flowers, and a dessert whipped up using a whole vanilla bean. On these lucky nights, I feel kept, known, and loved. I'm free to arrive as the worst physical version of myself—think sports bra, ratty sweats, and an unfortunate hair situation—yet I'm treated like a queen. Sarah's brand of hospitality plucks the very strings of my heart. I always count it a gift.

Though I still have some of that in me, most times I fall more on the side of "nope." Blame my kids or my house or my age. I don't know. Blame my life, which gets more peculiar by the year. For whatever reason, I don't pull off a fancy-pants dinner soiree quite like I used to. (If only I could remember this about myself.)

And now, to illustrate this truth, a play in three acts, the whole of which took place within the past year.

Act I

A guy named Seth came to town to visit the jail with Cory and stayed in our home. We had many mutual friends and had interacted online for a couple of years. I felt like I knew him, but I didn't actually. This made him a prime target for my dormant hostessing mania. There was no question that I would cook something special while he was with us. Here's where the trouble began, because though I could have made any number of familiar, perfectly delicious dishes, I tricked my mind into thinking special needed to mean interesting, which meant, apparently, it needed to be something I was not super adept at making. I settled on Jen Hatmaker's pad thai.[1] I'd made it once before, and we had slurped it up, denouncing takeout for life.

I'm still unclear about what went wrong the second time, but I'm comfortable shifting the blame to Jen, because what fun is a good cooking disaster without a long-distance scapegoat? Yada, yada, the house reeked of fish sauce, the noodles were somehow both burnt and soggy, and, later that evening, our dear houseguest, whom I now consider a dear friend, probably thanks, in part, to our shared trauma, confessed that his digestive system had staged an emergency coup.

All of this, when I could have just made soup.

Act II

Two months later, my sister and nephew were visiting. Spoiler alert: I hadn't learned my lesson. Let me offer the disclaimer that I don't often get to indulge palates as adventurous as my own. My family has learned to roll with the punches of my culinary tomfoolery, but beyond them, I try to rein it in when I'm feeding anyone whose underwear I haven't laundered. Seems like a fair litmus test. As you can imagine, as the older sister by five years and the washer of many loads of laundry throughout our growing-up years, Keisha fell tidily into my Zone of Reckless Abandon.

I decided to make pho. (This is where you are keenly identifying what I could not. International noodles + Shannan Martin + company = imminent doom.) I chopped and diced well beyond the bounds of good common sense. Rachael Ray would have barked disapproval at the amount of the prep time required. I made a special trip across town to the Asian market for fresh bean sprouts. I stocked up on sambal oelek. All for naught. It didn't matter that I'd made the soup a few times before to rave reviews and requests for thirds. When it came to the even slightly inflated pressure of cooking for my own sister, I choked . . . on noodles the consistency of rice pudding.

Even the unsuspecting, adventurous-eating two-year-old pushed it away.

Act III

Mere weeks after our pho misfortune, Cory and I were invited to the home of a new couple in our neighborhood. We chatted for a while in their living room, then moved into the kitchen, where Grant made some kind of magical pour-over coffee and set a kettle of water to boil for his wife and me. "We don't need to complicate it," he had said when he invited us. "If we get hungry, we'll figure something out. I just want to get to know you. That's the point. It's really pretty simple." Hours into our time together, he popped a pan of popcorn and sprinkled it with salt.

I walked home that night with a clearer understanding of what hospitality can look like, if we're willing to surrender our pride. Hosting friends in our homes can look bountiful, and some of us truly delight in planning every detail down to the fancifully shaped ice spheres. But it doesn't have to. When we say, "There is room here for you," the food, the décor, and the condition of our floors are small potatoes. When we say, "Come, sit next to me," it's our souls that are most hungry. Maybe the extra bag of chips in the pantry is all we need to fuel the conversation and seal our hearts. Maybe our definition of *bountiful* is itching to be stretched.

I poked around on social media recently, asking questions and taking notes. I wanted to know how we really feel about hospitality and what holds us back from stepping into it more often with more confidence.

Here's a sampling of what I learned, though, in most cases, it was stuff I already personally felt. For the most part, I wasn't learning as much as I was nodding along.

- Many of us are introverts (Hi! Me too!), and we've allowed ourselves to believe this lets us off the hook of inviting others into our homes.
- We all hate small talk.
- We think our homes aren't big enough.

- We fear judgment.
- We don't think we're good enough at cooking.
- It's hard to juggle small kids (naps, bedtimes, general chaos) and company.
- Parents of kiddos with special needs feel particularly on the far edges of this conversation.
- Single people aren't quite sure where they fit in the hospitality conversation and long to be included in the fiasco of family.
- Social anxiety is more common than we think and often more crippling than we know.
- Control is a beast that won't leave without a fight.
- Vulnerability is a muscle we aren't used to flexing.

For all the hang-ups we tossed into our shared, virtual pot of anxiety stew, there were also loads of helpful ideas. One commenter reminded us that hospitality isn't limited to our homes. "Start by inviting a friend to a park, and bring a thermos of tea."

A young family raising two kids with special needs said they shelved their anxieties by inviting families facing similar challenges. In doing so, they avoid the struggle of explaining the dynamics in their home to people who might not readily understand, and they cash in on the massive bonus of creating community with others who often feel similarly sidelined.

Another friend shared that her experiences with receiving hospitality from different cultures, where the preparation is part of the party itself and everyone pitches in, have helped relax her own methods.

Scrolling through hundreds of comments and e-mails, the central thread was clear. We are afraid to be rejected for who we actually are, so we either bail out entirely or crank it into entertainment overdrive, trying to wow our way around authenticity.

What if we each decided to go first and be the hostess we long for? Think for a minute about the times you've felt most at home, most comfortable and free. Scour the details. Was the floor freshly mopped? Did you swipe the baseboards with a white glove and Instagram the results? Did you pull out the refrigerator vegetable bins, checking for withered lettuce or slimy cilantro, ready to hurl stones? Did your host ask you to leave and not return until you were more smartly dressed? Did you pull out a scorecard and rate the meal? Were you positively disgusted by the antics of normal kids being their normal, dysregulated kid selves?

I'm guessing not.

What probably happened is that you felt listened to. Noticed. Included. Renewed. Accepted. You probably laughed a lot, and maybe you cried. You recognized a no-pressure zone when you saw it.

Bingo. That's our way forward.

We have deceived ourselves into thinking hospitality is more about the house than the humans. In reality, it's just the background noise to the real meat and potatoes of connection. If we can keep this reminder taped front and center, we might find ourselves falling willingly, happily even, into a new rhythm of belonging.

It doesn't have to begin with inviting strangers into your

home, or making Pioneer Woman's epic sloppy joes for six of your favorite incarcerated friends (though with any luck it will eventually evolve to that place, because Jesus knows how to point our eyes directly at him—and because Ree knows joes).

It can start with two hours, a tea kettle, and the affirmation that freshly baked scones outrank hygiene.

If you're more of a planner, pick a day of the month, or even (gasp!) a day of the week. Now, all you need to do is find some comrades and crack open a jar of salsa.

It can start with inviting people over at the last minute and insisting they wear stretchy pants. These eleventh-hour gatherings defined my childhood, shoring up the base of what I still believe to be true: we're better off when there's no time to sweat the details. It totally takes the pressure off.

My family regularly fielded and extended lunch invitations after church as I was growing up. "Just come!" they'd say. "Bring whatever you have!" We rarely ate out. Why would we have wanted to? The life in Christ I cut my teeth on was a long kitchen counter laden with odd feasts—pork chops and push pops and government cheese. It was always delicious, and there was always a place for me. Is it too much to dream of a last-minute lunch revival? Seems like such a sweet and simple place to start.

From there, we can cast the net even wider. What if we practiced our skills on people who already love us no matter what, then dared to believe they vastly outnumber those who don't? What's the worst that could happen?

Awhile back, after fending off a dozen little demons on my

shoulder telling me I shouldn't bother, I made a last-minute phone call to a woman I barely knew and invited her to join me. She said yes on the spot, audibly sighing as she shared that she had been feeling so alone. We've all been there before, staring into a foreseeable future of relational gloom before being lifted out by the prospect of being seen for all we are and loved anyway. Let our past hurts light the way as we search for those waiting to be included.

We pay attention, squeeze the life out of our fear, and wave each other in. Over time, we find ourselves believing good enough is good enough and the slow cooker is our friend.

I don't have a list of tips to offer. If you ever stay at my house (and I hope you do), I won't have a basket of individual toiletries by your bed, as every woman's magazine would advise. My gift to you will be clean sheets on the bed of a kid who has been temporarily displaced from his or her bedroom. If you come for dinner, there's a good chance I'll be serving Aldi pizza or some iteration of tacos—taco bowls, taco soup, slow-cooker pork tacos. Oh, and we only have water to drink.

We are pilgrims, it's true. But Christ is right here next to us, bumping elbows under the Target umbrella, sucking sauce off his fingers, and laughing at our jokes. He's shown us the way.

Just come.

Bring whatever you have.

Spread it around.

Chapter Nine

Searching for Your People

It happened near the kitchen pantry cabinet, somewhere around 3:05 p.m. on an average Monday. Silas had come home with a hitch in his britches about who-knows-what, so rather than smothering *him* with kisses first as planned, I pivoted to Ruby, who was getting ready to pour herself a bowl of Peanut Butter Cap'n Crunch. (Sugar cereal is a totally acceptable peaceful resistance, in case you haven't heard.)

Friends under the age of forty, I am here to warn you in advance about "the pivot."

It sounds innocent enough, doesn't it? Almost graceful, like something you do if you're resilient, emotionally flexible, and vaguely athletic. Unfortunately, I rival the athleticism of a block of parmesan, I resist last-minute changes, and when I tried to sub Ruby in as my first hug of the afternoon, I threw my back clean out.

I thought I had thrown my back out before, but now I know the other times were only drills. Now, I scoff at the younger me with her thrown-out back.

I shrieked, clutching my lower spine, and somehow hobbled to my bed, where I tried to laugh it off with the kids in a shaky attempt at delusion. I told myself if I just lay flat for a few minutes with Siley's Minions ice pack, I would be fine. I would still make it to Bible study with my pan of brownies.

Short story long, I was not okay.

I did not make it to Bible study that night, nor did I make it anywhere other than to the edge of despair for the next four days. I could not sit. I couldn't get comfortable in bed. Cory practically had to carry me to the bathroom, and I usually cried on the return voyage.

Hand to heart, I worried I had fractured my spine. I thought the pivot might have triggered a spontaneous, undiscovered form of cancer, and it was already metastasizing. Haunted by the thought of a novel I'd read years ago about a young girl whose mother was in an iron lung for her entire childhood, I imagined my kids feeding me orange slices two or ten years into the future, showing me grainy pictures of all the events I had missed.

Late into the night I moaned, "I don't know what to do," only interspersing it with the occasional, blanket apology, "I'm sorry." I'm not even sure who I was saying it to. Cory? Myself? Humanity? Never had my tea kettle, my good humor, or my out-of-state family felt so far from reach.

On day three, I posted a picture on Instagram, referencing my situation in passing. More than anything, I was paying tribute to Cory. His annual jail ministry banquet was set for the following day, which made it the busiest week of his year, and that's without taking into consideration that he was left doing every solitary thing around our house, for our children, and for his vegetative wife. His plates were spinning, and I, the most fragile of all, was profoundly grateful.

Twenty minutes after publishing the post, a comment popped up from Lydia, a local woman I'd only met once before. "Can I bring you dinner tonight?"

These six words undid me. My instinct was to message back, "We're fine, but thank you for offering!" (We have already discussed my natural, prideful aversion to receiving help.) But then I failed at rolling from my left side to my right side without assistance, and I remembered that nothing about me, us, the contents of our refrigerator, the number of hours in Cory's day, or the relentlessness of my kids' hunger was "fine."

I wrote back, "Dinner would be a huge blessing. I'm speechless over here . . . and also crying."

Despite my insistence that we're easy to please and I didn't want her to go to any trouble, she arrived later that evening bearing a stack of magazines, a gourmet meal, and a home-made cake with a separate little jar of freshly toasted coconut. (If it took throwing out my back to finally live my childhood *Bread and Jam for Frances* fantasy, with all her fancy side dishes, toppings, and extra creature comforts, it was almost worth it.) The point is not that she brought smashed ginger carrots with lime and the most delicious brussels sprout salad this side of Eden, but that she revealed herself as one of my people at a time when I needed support most.

Lydia was only the beginning.

When my family first dove into neighborhood life, we weren't prepared to fall headfirst into a pit of deep loneliness. It was a confusing beast. More than ever before, our lives were in the thick of the lives of other people. Our house was full and loud. We were learning what it meant to live with our door easy on its hinges. It felt, some days, like there were people *everywhere*. But our bodies were weary and our hearts felt unattended to. In a brand-new place, we were without close connections built on sustained history. I was surprised by how long we would feel adrift.

Dietrich Bonhoeffer, who spent years in the desolate confines of a prison cell, wrote, "It is Christ's will that [man] should be thus isolated, and that he should fix his eyes solely on him."[1]

Sometimes following Christ means our relationships might be chipped up, or even shattered. It means a measure of rejection. This relational exile hovering just past our reach is one of the ways we're bound to suffer.

God allows us to feel the occasional burn of isolation not only because he wants to rescue us, but also because often, in order to recognize the ache of those around us, we first have to feel it for ourselves.

And so, we waited it out. We relented to the inevitable pruning of our personal relationships. We watched some things die and gave ourselves permission to really feel the loss. We drew nearer to each other and uncovered a better understanding of the nearness of God.

Then, just when we were beginning to get cozy in this strange relational atmosphere, other lonely humans began to emerge from the landscape, taking us by surprise. "Our people" were right here, hiding in plain sight. Relief arrived a little at a time, a leaky faucet dripping onto parched earth. And then, the week of my spinal discontent, the floodgates opened, gushing compassion. (It's also possible the love had been there all along and it took being benched on the sidelines of my own life to really *see* it.)

For days I had despaired that I might miss the jail banquet, certifiably one of my favorite nights of the year. It was a race against time, and I tried to remain optimistic that I wouldn't have to be carried in by two former inmates.

The forecast, however, looked grim. This unwelcome state of utter dependence had completely unhinged my pride. I felt useless. Scared. My Ziploc ice pack of frozen peas had turned into a demoralizing paste. Twitter, my only companion during school hours, was busy feeding me its usual steady stream of global outrage. The kids prayed fervently for my healing, wondering out loud why God wasn't doing anything about it.

And then, I felt myself being lowered through the roof.

It wasn't instantaneous, as I would have hoped. It didn't happen like it did back in the church of my childhood, where, if the afflicted mustered up enough faith, healing would descend from the rafters, knocking people over and making folks dance. No. The Spirit of God blew into my home and my heart through his ordinary kids, the ones he had named as my neighbors. Some of my saints and angels were people the church might judge for various perceived offenses. (To that, I have learned to say, the church does not deserve them.)

Here's how healing happened:

My friend Kim, a woman I met the week we moved to town, showed up, laced my shoes onto my feet, helped me hobble to her car, and drove me to the chiropractor. She didn't comment on my woeful physical state or even shoot any pitying glances my way. Instead, she made me laugh and stuck around for a while after she brought me home, clueing in to the fact that I craved meaningful human contact and helping herself to a doughnut.

Jennifer, a woman who entered our lives several years ago when we temporarily cared for her granddaughter, sent me this text message: "I saw on Facebook your back is out? I have a great massage lady who does house visits. Can I send her to you tomorrow? I'm paying for it. Love you!"

Lisa, who at the time lived at the neighborhood work release center, walked over to check on me during the one hour of free time she had that day. Once here, she made a pot of coffee for herself and kept me company in my favorite way, by sharing the mundane details of her own ordinary life. Later that evening, I realized she had somehow, with the stealth of a street magician and at the speed of sound, folded the load of clean laundry that had sat ignored in my laundry room for days.

Becca, my favorite coffee-shop companion, showed up unannounced with hot chicken soup from the deli, chips and salsa, and a loaf of cranberry bread, each item a testament to her keen attention to relational detail.

While my banged-up body was being mended by God himself, my hope was being restored by the miracle of unlikely community he so lavishly and unexpectedly poured out on me.

A handful of years ago I didn't know any of these women. Our lives intersected in some of the strangest and most haphazard ways. None of us perfectly align on paper. Yet they were the actual, physical presence of God at a time when I was at my lowest. They scooped me up in profoundly personal ways. They saw my need and did tangible, unfussy things to relieve it, ordinary deeds made extraordinary. Water turned to wine.

Their breezy generosity leveled me.

One of the things I'm asked about most often is how my family found our people. Here's how: as we continue to study our corner of the world, we find others near us wanting the same things we do. Voila! Our people. We can stop searching for the perfect fit. Instead, we can look around for the people already living near us and take them (as they take us) as is.

The truth is, my family is only now identifying who our people are, and the hodgepodge list taking shape never fails to make us smile. Loneliness is still a part of our mission, and I know God wants it that way. But we are not alone. He keeps showing up, disguised as a loner, a struggler, an outcast. He arrives in the shimmering middle of everyday life. His abundance most often crops up right in the middle of our lack.

Is it too much to imagine a life where help and companionship are literally just a door or two away? A friend of mine recently confided that she struggled to love or even just plain like one of her nearest neighbors who happened to have a large, unruly dog prone to mayhem. Over the years, she kept her distance, entertaining unkind thoughts about the dog and its owner. Though she's far too lovely a woman to act on any mean-spirited fantasies, she allowed herself to believe she didn't owe them the time of day. That's all there was to it.

Then, unspeakable tragedy rocked my friend's family. They were flattened by the sort of grief that seems to know no end. Would you like to guess who drew near to them in unexpected mercy? Emotionally bloodied and beaten on the side of her Jericho road, she was hoisted up and carried to safety by the one she least expected, the one, in fact, she believed was her suburban enemy.

The world would not feel so impossible if each of us committed to truly knowing five of our nearest neighbors. We wouldn't feel so alone if we would commit without expectation to the big-hearted drifters nearest us. This flies in the face of church small groups commonly arranged by demographics and shared interests, but I promise that the result can be a wonderfully diverse reflection of God's kingdom.

It's not similar socioeconomic status, life experience, or theological positions that bind us, after all. Rather, it's basic proximity and the inevitable nomad status known, eventually, by every one of us. God's sacrifice is made evident through the willingness of his children to recognize one another as eternal family.

All of it is certain beauty, and I'm not so sure anymore that these are even ashes.

Chapter Ten

Nachos by the Hour

It was a typical Tuesday when my neighborhood finally snapped awake. We'd been restless for a while, walking bleary-eyed through the occasional warmer days, grinning sleep-drunk and grateful before slinking back into hibernation when the sky returned to steel. Maybe it was the puffy clouds, or the fact that a seventy-degree day in early May in northern Indiana is measured on a weighted scale. Whatever the case, for the first time in months, everyone seemed to be outside.

Driving back from dropping my son Calvin off at tae kwon do practice, I spotted the two of them running down the sidewalk toward me, my heart surging with a familiar blip of relief. When one of my adult neighbor-friends steps back into the picture after an extended time away, it's often under bleak circumstances. The kids are different.

They chased my van, ponytails whipping, mouths wide, banging on my window before I had even turned off the engine. Their version of catching up was a freight train of crosstalk, a fight against chickadees, nuthatches, and each other for my attention. They filled me in on everything I'd missed when the world was frozen and quiet: moves, trouble at school, a freshly broken arm. "She broke it last week, and the next day she got popular!" one of them said, gesturing toward her friend's blue cast, already dingy looking and covered in ink.

The world was vibrant, scented green. It was only natural for our conversation to turn to summer, less than a month away. Summer plans are mythical in these parts, apparitions of overblown hope and pennies pinched flat. We wondered aloud whether their moms would let them go to the city pool with us, or if they'd even be around, since there was buzz about exotic months spent in Chicago, maybe a trip to Six Flags or to the beach up in Michigan.

"Yeah, *right*." They laughed, rolling their eyes, well aware of the wobbly wheels beneath good intentions like these. In the middle of schoolgirl chatter, they spilled a story of finding a "big needle" earlier in the week at the park a few streets over. "It was filled with meth," one of them said, her wide eyes framed by grown-out bangs, a dull, purplish brown.

I sighed, my eyes narrowing. "Did you touch it? Never touch it. Promise me." Just one week earlier I'd spent an hour at the same park, unsettled by the way it rattled with a quiet anguish.

No, of course not. They didn't touch it. They know better, these students of a different kind of life, where breaking your arm without crying means flash popularity and it's not unusual to already know about syringes filled with meth in fourth grade.

After twenty minutes, my mind drifted to the pot of stock

simmering on my stove top. It was five fifteen, and I had to be somewhere by six. The weeknight shuffle stops for no man, no child, no early crack of spring. The girls ignored my attempt at a polite exit and followed me inside, no invitation necessary. (Sometimes I offer hospitality as worship. More often it's wrenched from my hands by a God who wants me nearer and knows I need a nudge.)

The dinners I cook are a long-standing joke, not just with the two girls, but with most of the neighbors who have taken a seat at my island and love me enough to be honest. To be blunt, it has given me a complex and grown me up in important ways. Loving the people nearest me often means deferring to them, so I'm learning to plan more spaghetti and ground beef taco nights, just in case. I'm buying bags of Takis chips when they're on sale.

But that night, the soup I stirred was extra funky. I wasn't even sure how to pronounce it, and they were both highly intrigued and more than a little repelled.

We talked about this and that, the two of them as light and giggly as every ten-year-old should be. Without thinking a thing about it, I opened the fridge to grab another ingredient.

And they both lost their minds.

I've seen the show *Hoarders* before, though not on purpose. It doesn't strike me as dignified or even as a particularly helpful sociological study. It seems more like a cheap opportunity to use the poor, the estranged, and those suffering with mental illness as entertainment. Just one more way to normalize our own failures. "I'm not *that* bad."

It makes my stomach hurt.

Guess what else makes it hurt? Watching two young girls gasp over how much food I have in my fridge. Realizing I am a hoarder in my own socially accepted way.

Generally, when I detect even a shred of discomfort in the air, I do whatever I can to diminish it. Often, the fastest way to diffuse what I perceive as a mounting power imbalance is vigorous defensiveness. *I am not better than you. I do not have that much more. I am not wealthy. I am not spoiled. Trust me.*

That evening was no different. I found myself making excuses, which only made matters worse. "I got groceries two days in a row! We needed everything! People eat a lot of food!"

I got groceries.

Two days in a row.

We needed everything.

People eat a lot of food.

Meanwhile, they were still telling short stories about what they usually had in their refrigerators and how they had never seen a fridge that full. Not once. "Maybe they're that full at a restaurant, but I don't know . . ." one of them said.

Bearing witness to lack constantly exposes my abundance in ways I find inconvenient and uncomfortable, particularly since I'm inclined to believe, despite all the evidence closing in around me, that I still don't have enough.

———

Two winters ago I flew to Ecuador with Calvin, age ten at the time, in tow. We traveled with Compassion International as part of a small group of writers and longtime Compassion sponsors tasked with spreading the word about the work being done to release children from poverty in Jesus' name.

We arrived in Quito, "the land of eternal spring," exhausted, sometime after midnight. Still, sleep toyed with me, lurking just past my reach. I wasn't scared, nervous, or even particularly unsure. Just restless. Calvin's breathing quickly fell into the steady rhythm I have learned to listen for, but I was still making the incremental rotations of the insomnia-oppressed. Right side, stomach, left side, back, my eyes adjusting, pulling light from the darkened room and the city beneath us.

After an hour, I finally relented and prayed.

Here's the thing about me and prayer: I'm no good at it. I've carried this insecurity as long as I can remember. My prayers are fleeting. Desperate. Weak and uncertain, just like me.

Oh, I know how to tidy them up. I'm a wordsmith by nature. My favorite art book is a thesaurus, and I have learned to talk a good game. But for some reason, when it comes to prayer, I struggle. Once in a while the power of God rushes through my throat and it *feels* holy. Most of the time, it's more like this: "God, be near." And then I repeat it about twenty-eight times like some weird audio glitch. (Earlier today I looked at the clock, remembering a dear, young friend was in court. Though I'd been seized all day with a composed panic, this was the only prayer available to me in my hour of concern: "Lord Jesus, send help.")

Back on that late February night, perched on the equator, what filled my heart and my brain were the words our little church family says together each week, "The prayer Jesus taught us to pray," as we often say. Maybe because I was tired and jumpy with anticipation, I went rogue and paraphrased, something like this:

> God, your name is holy.
> You're in charge of the whole world and heaven.
> You give us all we need for today.
> You show us grace and ask us to do the same for others,
>   even when it's hard.
> Help us not to be chewed up by the world. Be our
>   protection against evil.
> Everything we see and know, all that we are belongs to
>   you.
> You alone have power. You get the credit for everything,
>   and it is good.
> Amen.

I repeated it until I fell asleep, knowing in my bones that the words were true.

We headed out the next morning into streets that stole my breath. Stone walls mortared with sweat and prayer were studded with sharp jags of broken glass. Wild roses tumbled over the tops and hung in bright clumps around us. There were scribbles of graffiti, wild dogs, and stray cats with skinny tails.

As we made our way up the coastline, my senses jotted notes. We feasted on roasted chicken and corn against a backdrop of bamboo homes teetering on stilts. We played tag in

90 percent humidity, my sweat-soaked T-shirt clinging to my back. There were llamas and pigs and freshly squeezed mango juice. I watched a young, shy mother smile as she spoke kind words over her two teenaged sons, choking them up over all the love they held.

At our first home visit a young girl's father greeted us, holding back the *lindo* rose-patterned curtain that served as the door to their dirt-floored, one-room home shared among five people, roughly the size of one of my bathrooms back in Indiana. "Our home is humble, but our door is always open," he spoke softly. His dreams were many—for a steady job, a better home, an improvement of his family's condition. For his three children he hoped they would one day become "professionals."

My time in Ecuador held a constant tension, not unlike the tension I carry here in my everyday life. *How do we really connect with those who have so much less? Is my presence offensive to them? Are there barriers between us I don't even see?* Our path through the city was a blurry line cut between kingdom and earth.

In another home, carved straight from the rocky side of a hill, eight kids spilled from its dark mouth and showed us how to thumb large kernels of dried corn from the cob. A hog groused in its pen just past the doorway, fattening up to be sold.

"What do you normally have for dinner?" one of us asked.

"Corn," they said. "Corn soup or corn cakes or just corn. We usually have corn." I couldn't help wondering, *What do they make of God's promise of provision? How are they satisfied with daily corn when I know for certain I couldn't be?*

On the humid coastline of Manta, we arrived at the Compassion center to hordes of smiling kids greeting us, two of them with a "video camera" they'd crafted from scraps of cardboard and carried red carpet–style.

The pastor of the center gathered us together under the tin-roofed, open-air pavilion. At the close of her welcome she prayed, "Lord, open the window of your heavens and pour out your blessings on these special people."

There is no faster track to humility than being blessed by those who have less. Her reminder was a yank from God himself, snapping me to attentiveness yet again that the blessings I have are colorless and anemic compared to the blessings he has for me. I'm a human. A middle-class, white American. I live in a place where most people struggle and where life leans toward survival. And I still keep getting it wrong. I keep wanting more and bemoaning what I already have.

God promises daily bread but, I'll be honest, sometimes I'm tired of bread. Sometimes the bread I'm sent just isn't the bread I want. I'd rather have peach cobbler with whipped cream. A chocolate croissant. I'd rather have loaded nachos and, by the way, daily isn't quite often enough. I'd prefer them by the hour.

All the while, I live surrounded by gaping need and the throb of longing.

Just this morning, on my quick walk home from the school, I ran into a friend of ours. He was beginning his workday in a shredded secondhand jacket, the untethered nylon flapping around his chest and arms in the breeze like broken wings. He would be logging the next ten hours with a local slumlord who knows an opportunity when he sees one. My friend, fresh out of prison, was also fresh out of options, food, and minutes on his pay-as-you-go phone.

He beamed just as he'd done for the past five days. "I'm the only one who showed up again today! Guess I'm the only one who wants to work!" Living knee-deep in deficit, he was doing what he could, proving his resilience in the stony face of a life he never asked for.

We ticked down the list of things he'd gathered from our church congregation and all he still needed. "I'd really like to have a DVD player, even though I don't need one. I got a TV already, but it don't get any channels. It's just that it would be nice to be able to watch a movie or something after work. But it's no big deal."

I walked the rest of the way home with his blue eyes burned into my heart, one more lens from which to see the world. Suddenly, my house was enough. My closet was enough. The two off-trend rugs pieced together in my living room were enough. The car with no AC or power steering that still got Cory to work every day was enough.

It is infinitely harder to fantasize about more for me when I have proximity with the poor. The ground beneath my feet is a regular slap in the face, one I fear I'll never stop needing.

I can't fix economic systems or eradicate an entire history built on the backs of people deemed unworthy of justice. But as a woman of great privilege, the least I can do in the face of my community's and this world's suffering is make peace with my daily bread. I will remember their context as well as my own. I will not look only to those who have *more* as the measure of what I deserve. I will not lament humble things, nor wish (insincerely, let's be straight) for a harder, grittier life. I will not exaggerate my position on either end of the spectrum.

I will stare it all down with gratitude, and I will call it good.

My neighbors don't need my false alliances or my greed. What they need is my promise to keep being human, in all its conflicted glory. They need me to stay thick in the tension with them, enduring the "cringey" moments that are sure to pop up, refusing the temptations to constantly long for more or to believe my offering is best. Both lies scaffold brick by brick into barriers between us. Neither serves my soul or my community.

I want the equation to balance. I'm more comfortable with a handful of prescribed answers I can trot out when needed. I want to guarantee I'll never inflict harm. I don't like being reminded of the work I still have to do, or the fact that I just forked over $122.18 for more food than we can possibly eat before it rots. I cannot explain why some of us have more while so many have less. It doesn't seem fair because it isn't fair. The eleven-year-old girl we sponsor in Guatemala recently wrote to us: "Pray that we would have food to eat. Pray for our crops." This is squarely, unmistakably unfair. The temptation to invoke God's blessing around my material abundance only highlights how little I comprehend about the scope of his goodness and the trajectory of his affection. When I believe excess is a blessing, I have forgotten my Jesus, who warned the wealthy but blessed the poor. He wants our hearts, our service, our willingness to throw our trinkets and dreams on the altar of better, lesser things.

So, what are we to do with all our miscategorized treasure? Every breath of Jesus and every groaning of his spirit is an invitation to spill it out onto the world that waits, parched and panting. We can't surrender what we don't have after all. We are invited to greater generosity, to a looser grip on our money and our things, to a more expansive belief that the earth really is the Lord's, and everything in it (Ps. 24:1). We want to live more generous lives. But it's so easy to push against the ambiguous line of "how much do I have to give?" in order to satisfy the biblical mandate to care for the poor. These are tricky questions only the Spirit can answer.

Luke 21 tells us about the poor widow's offering. We know the story well. But I confess, I always nodded along, secretly thanking my lucky stars I would never know what it's like to give everything I have.

One wintry Sunday this played out in real time right there on the wooden pew. Walking to church that morning, I'd shoved my hand into the front pocket of my jeans, looking for a ponytail holder, and instead found a tightly folded five-dollar bill. *Zing!* Is there a better feeling?

It's not that I needed it. No. It was obvious icing spread thick across the layer cake of my life. It was free money. Play money. I could spring for the chocolate chip cookie along with my tea at the coffee shop while I worked on Monday. I could buy a thick, glossy fashion magazine and pretend I was nineteen again. I could snap up a lip gloss. A new app. Who am I kidding? I could buy a Five Buck Box at Taco Bell and eat it in my minivan with the radio blaring.

I entered the sanctuary my customary two minutes late, sliding in along the side wing, rows away from my usual spot. A few minutes later, Amber slid in beside me, her cheeks flushed from the cold, her boots tattered, her self-worth dangling, as always, right on the brink.

During announcements, Mary shared that we were collecting money to help pay for the teacher's luncheon the following week. "Just add your donation to the offering plate," she'd said. *Well*, I reasoned, *I have already tithed for the month. I've done more than enough for the teachers. I was already on the list to help cook the food and serve it, for the love of Mary, Peggy, and anyone else who cared, including Pete.*

I did my best to ignore the five-dollar bill resting against my thigh. Nope. I wouldn't give it. It was my found penny, heads up and gleaming. It belonged to me—*my* blessing.

The offering plate came nearer while Rich, our song leader, sang his exquisite custom blend of gravel and stained glass into a single sputtering mic. When the plate reached Amber, instead of passing it directly to me, she sat it on her lap, reached into her purse, and emptied a sandwich baggie of loose coins. Metal on wood, the sound was unmistakable. It was my heart pounding, my eyes filling. It was remorse and release. It was part bargain, part surrender, part battle-torn hope. It was worship.

I pulled out my five and threw it in, a "tiny part" of my "surplus," as Jesus would say (Luke 21:4). And I knew he was right. Amber understood something that was still lost on me.

In so many ways, she was better for it.

And in all the other ways, she was my living, breathing, fidgeting-in-her-seat invitation to tear off a hunk of what I had and pass it around.

As we face a world of hurts, ever more familiar with its contours, may this be our offering—that we never lose our taste for daily bread and that we remain eager to share.

Lord Jesus, send help. Lord Jesus, make it so.

Chapter Eleven

Let's Stop Loving on
the Least of These

Last summer, a church showed up at the park across the street to serve the poor. They wore matching T-shirts and brought in bounce houses and a stereo system blaring Christian music. My family kept our distance for a few reasons, one being that we knew we weren't what they had in mind when they came. Setting up a day of fun for under-resourced kids sounds like a good enough idea, right? I've seen it done many times before and thought nothing of it. I've also eagerly taken part in similar events throughout my life, believing I was doing something good and worthy. But in the past, I was always the one who drove to a different part of town and set up the popcorn popper. I had never been the one to whom the carnival came. I'm still confused about why it made my stomach drop, or why it still doesn't feel like justice these many months later.

My low-income neighborhood seems to be a hot target for people trying to scam us—overpriced cleaning products, discounted utilities, this brand of religion, that one. It hasn't gone unnoticed that when people show up around here, they usually want something. Understandably, many of us have raised our guard, taping signs to our front doors and keeping the curtains drawn.

While sharing the hope of Christ is certainly not wrong, there's a better way to connect with overlooked people. It involves not just a loving gesture, but actual love that cannot be put on, taken off, or packed up at the end of the day.

Back in my youth group years, we participated now and then in door-to-door evangelism, which we called canvassing. It was presented as a way of putting legs to our faith, literally walking it out into the beaten-down world. It was a test, and though I hated every second of it, I hated failing worse. Even when it was optional, I volunteered. I knocked on doors in Southern Ohio trailer parks, my permed bangs lacquered with Aqua Net (lavender can). I knocked on doors of cobblestone cottages in Northern Ireland wearing a perpetually damp jacket.

I don't remember any banner encounters with the unsuspecting, unlucky few who answered, but I do remember the rush of relief when no one was home, or when they pretended not to be. We were taught that this was the way of demonstrating love to those bound for hell unless we intervened. We were sweaty-palmed evangelists, timid and afraid of rejection. I loathed the thought of putting someone on the spot. Rather than responding with gratitude, the people we sought to save tended to react with defensiveness, or even anger. Though I couldn't have put it into words then, I knew our methodology was askew. We boxed up the holiest of relationships and tried to shove it through cracked-open doors, handling the gospel like a box of encyclopedias with a three-month payment plan, detached, impersonal, the antitheses of the Jesus way.

Here's the other thing I never stopped to question: we typically gravitated to the shabbier neighborhoods. Our intentions weren't at all bad. We believed every person at his or her core needs Jesus. We believed he is the only fix. All this is true, but we quietly, almost invisibly, took it one step further. Somewhere in the subterranean layers of our souls, we believed physical poverty was in some way bound with spiritual poverty. Following this logic, we thought we'd find more takers in low-income areas. It was our fast track to task completion. So that's where we went.

We would never have had the gall to show up in a high-end subdivision or on the shaded streets of a quaint small town. It didn't cross our minds.

Just last week, I heard a guy on television talk about a neighborhood like mine. He furrowed his brow and looked earnestly into the video camera, his teeth bleached and arrow-straight, his hair expertly coiffed. "They're all so broken over there," he said with a wince, the sleeves of his black T-shirt taut across his biceps with the bottom half of a hipster-approved tattoo peeking out.

The whole thing rubbed me the wrong way, but not because his words were untrue.

He's right. We are all so broken over here.

But if I know anything, it's that he is too. I have to wonder, does even a shred of humility come across when we're the ones knocking on the doors of strangers or dragging portable air compressors and grills over the railroad tracks or setting up professional-grade equipment so we can shoot a video for our suburban congregation that casts us as inspiring urban heroes? I'm not talking about building trusted, sacrificial, long-haul relationships, learning nicknames and backstories, sharing our own. My concern is the obvious power imbalance at play when we feel at liberty to show up in a place we know little about, bearing a rescue no one asked for.

When it comes to loving the poor, the vast majority of us have no intention of doing harm. We want to take part in the holy work of God; we're just a bit bumbling and unsure. We're afraid of getting things wrong and, quite bluntly, we are just plain afraid. We've been taught to be leery of poverty, maybe even to judge it, which presents us with a conundrum since we know God tells us to figure it out. We want to help, but we don't know how, and the messages about how best to come alongside those who need our help are muddy. Too often, we tend toward rolling out a program when perhaps what every person needs most is a welcome mat, a place where they are known and welcomed and loved without expectation, no strings attached.

Just last week I sat with a woman currently navigating homelessness with her young family, doing her best to receive the help offered by well-meaning Christians, though it is rarely what she wants or needs. "We don't need someone's old clothes," she said, her voice crackling on the edge of tears. "We don't need people to pity us or tell us to trust in God. We need a smiling face. We want to know we're not alone. We want someone to listen, and to root for us." Every word of it made sense to me.

Here's what I'm learning to do, and I will warn you, it sounds so obvious you might think I'm being sarcastic. (No dice.) When it comes to sharing the light and love of Jesus with the world around me, I first think hard about how I prefer to be engaged. If the methods would cause me to feel defensive, unsafe, or even just annoyed, it is only fair to assume anyone else would react in the same way.

Do I feel loved when a stranger knocks on my door and asks if they can pray with me or tries to peddle their particular brand of faith? No.

Does it feel good when someone who barely knows me pries into my private life in a way that feels challenging, condemning, patronizing, or even vaguely judgmental? Absolutely not.

Do I like being held hostage in my own home, forced to either endure the intrusion or dismiss the visitor in a way that makes me feel like the bad guy? No, I do not.

Am I grateful when someone approaches me as a project or tries to foist their wisdom or theological superiority on me? Do I sense true and enduring friendship when someone comes at me with an agenda? No, no, and no.

Do I want anyone in the entire world, with one notable exception, to "love on me"? Um, no. Kindly, don't you dare.

I deeply need the church to put a sweeping, immediate halt to loving on people, particularly those whose bedhead we have never beheld or whose junk drawer we have not born solemn witness to.

I implore us. It is time. This is churchy-talk at its worst, a misappropriation of words meant to obscure the fact that we still have quite a lot to learn about the love of Jesus that saves through surrender. This quietly hierarchical lingo almost always conveys a single direction, and relationships are not paved with one-way streets.

Jesus said the poor will always be among us, not as a warning but as a promise. His life was a picture of the gift of their nearness. He chose to be with those most overlooked. He subverted the religious, then partied with those who didn't fit the mold of earthly esteem.

He wants the same for us, not as a test of our faithfulness but because he loves us too much to let us miss out. And he knows, as we practice proximity with those we think of as lacking, we will begin to see ourselves aligned, the chasm between us narrowed to the width of the street where we live.

Rather than clinging to this easy vernacular of "them" and "us," let's keep being broken together, slow to assume that certain people automatically need Jesus. Maybe they already have him. Maybe they just need a true friend. Maybe if we find ourselves compelled toward them it's because we need to be discipled *by them.*

The poor are everywhere, in every zip code. If we are serious about loving them, we have to put in the unsexy time it takes to discover who they are and what they need. Maybe a bounce house and hot dogs shared with people who really love them would be a true respite from the yank and shove of life. Regardless, love asks us to be ready to enter into their lives fully, not content with referring them to agencies for assistance but eager to take on their limp as we walk closely with them through trouble. Joining us at church or praying a prayer doesn't need to factor into the equation at all. In fact, what if we all made a pact to not invite anyone to church if we hadn't already invited them over for a meal?

"For I was hungry, and you fed me. I was thirsty, and you gave me a drink. I was a stranger, and you invited me into your home. I was naked, and you gave me clothing. I was sick, and you cared for me. I was in prison, and you visited me" (Matt. 25:35–36).

In other words, "I was a single mom, and you offered me a free night off. I was new to America, and you showed me around town. I was released from jail, and you bought me steel-toed boots for my factory job. I was racked with anxiety, and you listened without checking your phone. I was in jail, and you put money on my books for shampoo and a sports bra."

"I tell you the truth," Jesus said, "when you did it to one of the least of these my brothers and sisters, you were doing it to me!" (Matt. 25:40).

I wish I had a surefire plan for guaranteeing I would always get this right. I don't. I don't know how to ensure my good intentions will never make matters worse, further diminishing good people already short on respect.

But I'm certain of this: we need to be willing to be wrong. It's time for us to wear the humility of Jesus like a secondhand coat, ready to hear from people further along this road. We've got to stop insisting on our own way and believing we know best. As we commit to listening closely to the people around us, we need to invite correction and ask forgiveness when necessary.

We don't need a curriculum, a bulging missions budget, or a group rate on screen-printed T-shirts. We're probably better off without all that. God sent the Holy Spirit as our guide, along with sensory-rich bodies capable of discerning the reality splayed out around us.

Here's what I'm hearing these days from the Lord: *Love your neighbor, Shannan. Love them like you love your own children. Love them like I love you. Love them with hot soup. Love them with humility. Love them by trusting them with your own failures. Point them to me. Pray for them. Rub their backs while they cry. Give them fifty dollars and don't ask for it back. Cheer them on because life is terribly unfair. Bake them cakes from a box, and sing to them on their birthdays. Get to know the patterns of their lives so you can see when trouble has come to camp. Get involved. Give them rides. Let them buy your lunch sometimes.*

Real love takes time; its growth is slow and sustained. If we want to love the world around us—and Jesus warned often that this is half of what classifies us as his—we have to pass by each other, get a good, honest look, call it beautiful, and stick around.

———

St. Mark's United Methodist Church was built in 1888, a small sanctuary with two sections of carved wooden pews bisected by a short center aisle. Natural light filters in through a massive, gothic-shaped stained-glass window on the east wall. Somehow, the space manages to be both traditional and unfussy. It grows dearer to my heart, more sacred, with each Sunday spent passing the peace and praying with all who gather. I love it.

Over the years, new additions have been grafted onto the building. You can't miss the demarcations, each batch of brick slightly different than the one it's cobbled against. First there was a foyer, then upstairs corridors of classrooms, a small library, and eventually a sprawling northern wing complete with a gymnasium-like gathering space and a commercial-grade kitchen. Here, in Albertson Hall, the white-haired ladies, many of them friends for upward of fifty or sixty years, dutifully host annual rummage sales and cook funeral dinners for the saints as unto the Lord.

In keeping with our old-school Methodist roots, this is also where we hold carry-in lunches every couple of months. (I once entered my chicken and white bean recipe in a chili cook-off and didn't even place. This is how serious my mainline brothers and sisters are about food.) Once, when the elementary school across the street was desperately in need of a new playground, we held a pie auction after church to help them raise the funds. From across the room, we outbid one another and talked a good bit of smack. (I walked up the alley toward home that day the proud winner of five pies, because in the scheme of life, I don't want to have to choose between Caroline's peanut butter pie and Maxine's rhubarb.)

It was no surprise when a carry-in-style baby shower was proposed for Taylor, about to pop with her third son. She had made her way to us a few months earlier when her long-term boyfriend, Greg, began walking over from work release. Now, they were part of us, plain and simple. They shared their lives along with the occasional prayer concern during sharing time, their four-year-old son especially interested in laying claim to the microphone so that he could tell us again about the pizza place of his dreams where he one day hoped to work. Our small church body was itching to help meet some of their needs while showing them just how much they belonged.

The baby shower was an epic display of celebration, complete with miniature plastic baby bottle centerpieces and powder-blue streamers. By the time it was all said and done, it took three trips to get everything loaded into Taylor's hatchback.

The faithful men and women of my church, particularly the older generations, continue to school me in the ways of loving with open arms, being patient with discipleship, and extending personal care and affection to the few who wander our way.

As some of us were cleaning up after the party, Mary began her usual off-loading of leftovers. "Shannan, would you take some of these baked beans home?" and then, a split-second later, "Oh, I almost forgot. Cory doesn't eat beans."

I find it difficult to express why her words were so meaningful to me, so I'll just say that they stopped me in my tracks, and when I got home that afternoon, I went straight to my journal and wrote them down for safekeeping. I had no idea Cory's picky eating preferences were widely known among our church family. I'm not sure how Mary came upon the information, or why it stuck with her. The only thing that mattered was the understanding that we are *known*. Exactly for who we are.

All of us feels "least" in some way. Yet just like Greg, Taylor, and their growing family, we have been counted as worthy of time and attention by a small but mighty group of people who have felt the nearness of God and are eager to spread it around.

This is a snapshot of the beating heart of God, in close solidarity with us through the everyday details of life. He doesn't just visit us when we're praying or behaving. He doesn't waste his time harping on the cobwebbed corners of our lives that would benefit from some broad improvements. He's not our nitpicking great aunt who seems to come to town now and then only to express her disappointment.

He's mad about us. He causes the light to fall on the best of who we are, nudging us shoulder to shoulder toward better things when we get stuck. What he wants most is to be near us. So that's what he does. He stays close, pays attention, and, when necessary, settles in until we realize just how *with* us he really is. He is Jesus, God incarnate, inviting us to care for each other with the same tenderness and attention.

He is our friend Mary, making the world brighter in Albertson Hall as she wipes the counters with a soapy rag.

Part Three

Work Like
a Neighbor

Chapter Twelve

Contact Burns

Over the past year, Silas, our youngest, has become border-line obsessed with taking showers. This one falls under the parenting shorthand category of "a sensory kid." Hard pants—anything without an elastic waistband, also known as cold pants—are out. Anything smooth or aglow with lights is in. Water wins the world. When we send him to the shower, sometimes twice in one day, he stays until we make him leave, splashing around and talking to himself loudly enough that it drifts downstairs. I recently pressed him on why he loves showers so much, and he said, "It's just what grown-ups do!" As if he is obviously among us.

Si is our only extrovert. He's an epic chatterbox with a blooming pop-culture obsession. Recently, we caught wind of an elaborate telephone-shower game he dreamed up, inspired by the opening scene of Adele's *Hello* video and complete with the British accent. Unbeknownst to the rest of the family, like any good and nosy sister would do, Ruby camped outside the bathroom door and took notes. She came to us, giggling, and read her dutiful transcription of his one-sided telephone conversations.

"Hello? Yeah . . . I was on house arrest. Well, I got out yesterday."

His next call: "Hello? Hey, guys! Yes. I am in jail. I will be out soon, but I cannot go back to school until I'm nine and in the third grade."

On and on it went, the weirdest, sorriest succession of fake phone calls, all laced with the sort of urban drama I never imagined my child would understand, much less use as a backdrop for imaginative play.

We howled with laughter.

The next morning, though, I couldn't stop crying as we were once again dealt the sort of bad news that has become all too familiar.

Life has become a long, shocking reckoning of all that I do not know. My young kids grow tall and secure under a fortuitous canopy of fierce love and secondhand pain. Most of the guests around our table have felony convictions. And I've become a lay expert on addiction, adept at translating the language of acute disconnection and shame.

When Jessie showed up at our door, desperate to get clean, I didn't have a clue what to do, what I was signing up for, or how to behave. I wasn't versed in what to say, or even which emotions to show. *Is this the time to be visibly worried? Angry? Upbeat? Should I try to cry a little?* I wasn't sure, so I put clean sheets on the bed, heated her a bowl of broccoli cheese soup, and prayed for a miracle.

She had disappeared suddenly from our lives two weeks before, and we knew it wasn't good. The previous winter I had driven her to her restaurant job most mornings, cataloguing her fears of relapse. Addiction was a noose hanging loose around her neck, just waiting to be caught. I watched her glance behind her shoulder, constantly measuring the distance between herself and the prowling wolf. Her cheeks rounded out as she added weeks and then months to living clean, but her anxiety didn't seem to settle. *Why?* I wondered often. *Isn't she out of the woods?*

Straining to move forward, she found a new place to live and began hunting thrift stores for cute living room curtains, a sister after my own heart. She complained that none of her old clothes fit anymore, the waistbands sinking teeth into her sobriety. One afternoon as she sucked down cigarettes on my front porch, berating her weight gain, I suggested she take up walking.

"Walking? Like, just, *around*? For no good reason?" Her laugh was a finger wagging at all I didn't know about her life.

She kept on loving me.

She told stories that still make me nauseous, some that still make me blush. One summer night she called as I was driving to Target for another pair of shoes I didn't need, and she begged me to turn around and pick her up. When she pointed to the coral sandals, saying she liked them best, my decision was made. She had wormed her way to the core of my heart. I was overcome with love and optimism for her. Sometimes secondhand smoke is the fragrance of Christ himself, and I pull a long drag.

The night she turned up unannounced, it took every shred of my will not to stare at the scabs dotting her hands and arms, a roadmap of shame. Her cheekbones were a revelation, jutting up from the landscape of a Jessie I didn't recognize. I didn't know her as a size two with darting vision. I had never known her strung with paranoia like a marionette doll, her movements no longer fluid or controlled.

This was my first exposure to a world I had only heard about, and I was already homesick.

The weeks that followed tracked a jagged trail of events where I handled the delicate anatomy of reality with my own shaking hands. I screamed clumsy, unfamiliar words and fell headlong into her despair. I wasn't sure what was real anymore, but I knew my heart was breaking. Death circled quietly overhead, unmoved by my grasp of the New Testament and my internal playlist of Christian songs. Jessie left after a couple of weeks with no bad blood between us, just the gaping wound from a beast she couldn't tame.

Not long after, she sent me two close-up snapshots of herself, smiling and clear-eyed. She was in rehab, half a state away. The photos were old, but I knew they could also be a flash into the future. I stuck both pictures in my Bible, shuffling them around as bookmarks, staring at her pretty face every now and then and clinging to belief. Sometimes, what holds us together is an unlikely, tangible thing, a glossy slip of paper, and the faith that it won't be lost.

Addiction, Jessie's along with so many others', takes up more of my mental space than I ever imagined it would.

Journalist Johann Hari wrote, "I have been turning over the essential mystery of addiction in my mind—what causes some people to become fixated on a drug or a behavior until they can't stop? How do we help those people to come back to us?" In his quest for answers, Hari came upon some research that argues that addiction is less about a chemical hook and more about human isolation. Nurture over nature. "If we can't connect with each other, we will connect with anything we can find—the whirr of a roulette wheel or the prick of a syringe," Hari wrote.

"So the opposite of addiction is not sobriety. It is human connection," Hari concluded.[1]

I must have read that line fifteen times to the imagined sound of shattering glass. I wanted to break something. I can handle the biological components of addiction; I've made some peace with this. But I have held hands with too many beloved people through the flames to find this new conclusion comforting. I have sat so closely, stayed so near. It's not about me—it never was—but I cannot stomach the thought that addicts essentially die of loneliness while my skin is still burning.

It's two years after Jessie's initial relapse, and I never hear from her anymore. My attempts to reach out are pinging around somewhere in the digital air. I look at her photos most days, still terrified addiction will kill her, and pleading it won't.

In the life I imagined for myself and my family, the hardest questions would wait until we were ready. Yet, here we are anyway, dodging shrapnel and throwing off our own sparks while we tend to the mundane necessities of life, opening and closing cabinets, folding socks, tackling dinner on the fly, begging for Minecraft time, hacking away at Barbie's polyester hair. The crumbs of life are the guts of life, and this is life now, with one foot on our swept floors and the other in the mud.

Last fall, as the farmers hauled their harvest in for the winter, I watched anxiety crop up in Cory like crabgrass across our stable, middle-class life. It showed up inconspicuously at first, an anomaly, like one leaf turning too soon while the rest of the tree is still green. *Maybe he's just tired. Maybe it's the kids. Maybe it's allergies. Maybe (probably?) it's me.*

A few years before, when he traded in his suits, ties, and daily shaving for a job as the full-time chaplain of our county jail, it seemed too good to be true. Now, he spends each day with men who hold the keys to God's kingdom. They lead him to the feet of Jesus. He counts them as his best friends.

He also listens to endless stories of trauma, pinballing from loss to loss across decades that span from birth to life and back again. The bulk of his waking hours are now spent absorbing the torment of his brothers, swallowing it down along with plastic spoonfuls of high-sodium macaroni or mystery gravy.

As far as jobs go, he's sure he won the prize.

But no one can stand near lives that are constantly on fire without their own skin being scorched. It took awhile for us to connect the dots, *his* contact burns hanging hidden inside the walls of his big heart like flyers on a telephone pole, one stapled right on top of the other, the ink blurred by the rain, the edges curling over time.

We figured it out, he enlisted professional help, and in a culture where mental illness remains deeply stigmatized, he now looks for opportunities to talk about his new diagnosis, pulling his chair up to this new table of tender empathy.

Survival will require support from other humans along the way. Our trials won't always be dramatic, and they probably won't involve meth. I'm here to raise my right hand and promise there is no such thing as a too-small gesture of genuine kindness. It doesn't exist. Any sacrifice drawn from a well of compassion is an act of everyday heroism, and I should know.

In the first days after Ruby was handed to me by her birth mom, as I was feeling every inch an inadequate basket case in my wreck of a kitchen, I remember peeling the foil off of a string of meal deliveries from our Sunday school class and pledging allegiance to Someone Else's Pasta. We ate our weight in lasagna.

There's no such thing as a minor blessing. But seeking to ease the burden of a world gone wacky will often stretch our limits of what is comfortable, launching us straight into the sorrow and mess we have prayed fervently to avoid.

Part of me wishes there were another way. I wish I could pass out popsicles and promise our safety and comfort will remain flawlessly intact. As we push into the forgotten corners around us, there will be times we'll think it's too hard, or that we aren't cut out for the sort of heartache that robs us of sleep. We might be tempted to believe we can't put our sweet kids through it, that they don't deserve it. I wish I could reassure us that God just wants us to be happy. I wish complexity and risk were not promised us, that we could always pay up in spaghetti with meat sauce.

The question then is, where do we choose to stand? How close to the flames? Henri Nouwen wrote,

> Here we see what compassion means. It is not a bending toward the underprivileged from a privileged position; it is not a reaching out from on high to those who are less fortunate below; it is not a gesture of sympathy or pity for those who fail to make it in the upward pull. On the contrary, compassion means going directly to those people and places where suffering is most acute and building a home there.[2]

I have friends who quite literally have built homes in broken places. I also have friends who build these homes of compassion in different ways. Counted among our most trusted confidants are those who live in rural settings but jump one city over to slowly build trusted relationships with those living in a homeless shelter. We know a couple who live in an upscale subdivision but spend most of their free time inside the jail. We have friends who choose low-income schools, some who choose dying churches, and others who keep the guest bed made up with clean sheets for anyone who might need it.

Camped out at the margins, however it might look, we are guaranteed to find little-known heroes trudging beneath impossible burdens. It could be drug addiction, relational chaos, or the heel of the system. It might be a chronic illness, a special-needs child, the ache of single parenting, a run-in with the law, a merciless bout with depression, church-related judgment, or the cumulative effects of being invisible. It could be a thousand different things. Once seen, we can ignore it, or we can march straight to the heart of it, chasing kinship through the fumes of white-hot trouble floating up from the asphalt.

Reality check: we won't be able to fix any of it.

But our resting temperature will rise, just as two clasped hands trade heat until they equalize.

We keep failing our friends and our friends keep failing us. We take turns, trade seats. We hold their lives to the light and combust with the heat of our own glaring poverty. Slowly, often imperceptibly, we drag each other back out into the noonday sun, where all the filth is exposed and there's no time to find shade. We teach and learn and *I hate the ways we keep screwing things up.* But the point was never perfection. The point was community—sharing a messy life, in slivers and in shards.

A neighbor boy showed me his broken pinky finger at the bus stop one morning. He was pretty proud of his injury, waving it around with all the false bravado you might expect from a kid about to tip into adolescence, trying not to wince. I stood there wishing for two strips of tape to hold it steady against his ring finger while it healed.

That's what we are. That's what we do.

Sometimes I'm the sideways pinky. Sometimes it's you.

Emmanuel came for all of us, to walk in my pain and in yours. He came to see it for himself, to touch it, to redeem it and call it beautiful. He came to show us the high honor of skin thickened from exposure yet tender to the touch.

My friend Ginni once said, "Preventing poverty promotes world peace." I haven't quite figured out a bang-up solution for doing this. Until we've kicked it, we'll stay near the flames, enduring it together and trusting God is with us.

We breathe in the truth. There is no good, only loved. Only trying. Only forgiven.

In and out. On and on.

We are all still very much alive.

Chapter Thirteen

We All Are Mothers

It was the dog days of summer, and our oldest son, Robert, was in the throes of romantic drama once again. I had stopped by the house he shared with his girlfriend, a woman I dearly love, to drop off a baking dish they were borrowing. It didn't take long before I was sucked into the details of their ongoing dispute. They are truth-tellers, incapable of holding back their feelings, yet understanding the value of counterweighting hard truths with kindness and humor. But both of them had unhealthy relationship patterns born of traumatic pasts. It seemed drama was never more than a day away.

Due to entanglements with the criminal justice system, both were saddled with the many requirements that keep people in their situation down, rather than lifting them up. Our conversation turned to their kids (all from prior relationships), and I remembered Robert had been court ordered to attend parenting class (along with anger management, mental health screening, substance abuse programming, probation, random drug testing, and other demands, many of which were entirely unrelated to his case, but I digress). I brought the required classes up quite casually, as is my way. The impulse to be nonchalant and positive surged through my amygdala, and I carefully crafted my case.

"When Robert starts parenting classes, you should go too!" I told his girlfriend, making sure my face was bright and casual. "I would totally do it if I had the chance. Being a mom is the hardest thing I've ever done. I need all the help I can get." She remained noncommittal and the conversation moved on.

A few weeks later, their relationship came to an abrupt and irrevocable end. (I'm still sad about it.) The little we know about life for those society hates can be summarized as this: it's stressful for everyone. Relationships between two people straining just to survive are often tenuous, prone to breaking without warning.

A month later, I got this text from Robert. "Hey mom. I got us signed up for our parenting class. It starts next Tuesday."

(Insert record scratch.)

My casual comment about how I would totally take the class if I could had somehow lodged in Robert's long-term memory. And this is how I accidentally signed up for a ten-week, court-ordered parenting class with my twenty-two-year-old son.

When we showed up together on the first night, I saw that the rest of the class consisted of young singles or couples (each attendee is invited to bring a guest, so, obviously, most bring the person they coparent with as opposed to, say, their actual parent). Most also had their young children in tow, since there was a family meal and craft time, along with separate programming for children.

Close your eyes and try to imagine this scene, where the two teachers, both middle-aged, white men, did their best to politely discern why Robert and I were there together. We didn't come close to fitting the couple mold, even though we were both grown adults and he towered over me at six feet four inches. But when Robert attempted to relieve some of the underlying tension by barking out, at his customary maximum-decibel level, "She's my mom!" I sensed the two of them still had more questions than answers.

Nevertheless, we signed on all the lines, paid our dues, and spent the next ten Tuesdays eating beans and hot dogs, making homemade play dough and paper-bag puppets, reading children's books together, playing Chutes and Ladders, and attending a carnival.

Disclosure: I loved all of it. Since we adopted Robert when he was nineteen years old, I had missed his entire childhood, and then some. Getting a chance to reclaim lost time through some of these milestone parenting moments was special in a way I wasn't prepared for. It was also hilarious, at times, and Robert did his best to weasel out of the activities each week. But it was clear to me that it filled a small place inside him too. God redeems in the best, weirdest ways.

After dinner, the adults filed into a classroom where we sat together week after week receiving instruction, watching cheesy videos set in the eighties, completing old-school worksheets, and humbling ourselves in necessary ways. Going in, my hackles were raised. I remembered how embarrassed and defensive I had felt fifteen years ago when I'd had to sit through an all-day driving school after one too many traffic tickets. This was on a whole new level. Most of our group had been deemed by the courts as people who were struggling with parenting. I could only imagine how that felt. So I'd prepared myself ahead of time to be outraged over the insensitivity of the instructors or the condescending atmosphere. I even planned to take notes in a small notebook and was ready to bang out an emotional exposé if the situation warranted it.

What I found instead was the surprise of true community, richly diverse and utterly unfussy. It didn't take long to discover who was shy, who was loud (I'm looking at you, Robert), who was combative, who was timid. Some stayed pretty checked out. Others of us began dropping small facts about our lives, our stories, and the kids we were raising. A young woman, exuberant without exception, came to class one evening with her thick, black hair twisted into an elaborate crown atop her head, Dum Dum suckers spaced evenly through the plaits of the braid that held it all in place. She was a charming, comedic Statue of Liberty there in our midst. When a classmate answered a question correctly, she would reach up, remove a sucker from her crown, and toss it to him or her. In the unexpected parade of court-appointed parenting classes, she was our clown and our resident Kiwanian rolled into one, throwing good will around by the fistful.

My assumptions were destroyed as we sat together each week, students of parenting and life. There was no discussion of the mistakes that had led us there, just the prevailing sense that we were all in it together. What drew us near was a central force, a shared thread. We were parents with room to grow.

As the world gets more confusing and trickier to navigate, my role as a mom rockets up the chart of significance. And before I say another word let me be perfectly clear—all women are mothers.

We are life-givers, each of us, in ways both wild and vast. Our title as mother isn't defined by biology or science. It can't be measured in centimeters or the arc of a curve. Mothering is the thing *all* women do, with the small and big kids under our care, the neighbor boys up the street, our students, our grown nieces, the children we can only hold in our hearts, and the ones we don't even know yet to hope for. What I'm trying to say is that none of us is off the hook here.

Humanity is crying out to be nurtured.

There are dozens of opportunities to do this during any given week, or even daily. It doesn't matter where you live, what you look like, how similar or different you feel from those around you. It doesn't matter if you work outside or inside the home, or whether you're in government housing or on a cattle ranch in Oklahoma. The question is, as always, are we paying attention?

Have we made ourselves available? The way we spend our love is the way we spend our lives. Do we care enough to love those around us as though we really belong to each other? And can we dare to believe these small gestures of specific care and well-timed warmth are enough to alter the path of mankind?

Here's a true story. One of the sweetest, safest, most

distinct memories I have from childhood is the day I was struck with a migraine, just before the bus was set to leave for a junior high basketball game, for which I was a cheerleader (a bad idea for someone with my skill set, but I'd rather not talk about it). I was physically wobbly, with pain creeping over me like a spider in the dead of night, and all I wanted was to be tended to, safe and sound. The fact that my mom was at work and unreachable caused me more than a little emotional anguish. But my best friend Angie's mom, Sue, swooped in and grabbed the maternal baton right on time. I got over the headache, but I will never get over the relief of being tucked into clean sheets on her couch.

Sue didn't see me as someone else's sick kid. She took me in as her own, choosing compassion over convenience.

Mother Teresa famously said, "If you want to bring happiness to the whole world, go home and love your family." We gobble up her words, plastering them on signs and hand-lettering them onto notecards. We love them because they are beautiful. And profoundly true. But let's not forget, this is the same Mother Teresa who reminded us to "draw a wider circle" around who we consider family. Seen under the light of that truth, new meaning emerges. If we want our world to be better, we have to go out and love the people around us. We need to invite them in, as family.

Beginning to live as though there's no such thing as other people's children might be our most critical, significant contribution to the flourishing of our world. Simply believing this, however, is not enough, and sympathy without action is no more than wasted breath. Mothering is often physical, gut-wrenching work.

What do we believe our kids are owed? To what ends would we go to offer them protection, support, and love? Just this week, I have lost sleep over the heartache of one of my kids. I've sent e-mails, searched for outside support, indulged a few unhealthy fantasies involving the vigilante justice of a forty-one-year-old mama with a few bones to pick, and, *oh*, how I have prayed. I love my kids. There's not much I wouldn't do to make sure their needs are met. The dreams we have for our children—to know community and freedom, to grow in truth, to be safe and loved—must be available to all. We are lion-hearted mamas, every one of us, made to roar for the kiddos most closely within our reach.

Do you believe your children deserve nutritious food and plenty of it? A vibrant education? Lives free from discrimination and violence? Do they deserve basic kindness and respect? Do they deserve life itself, free from trauma and marginalization?

Assuming your answer is yes, let the same be said for all God's children. And *you* are uniquely positioned to work toward that goal in your ordinary place.

If you're a public-school champion, do everything you can to make that school better. This serves every sweaty, silly child in the building.

Are you a committed homeschool mom? You might be perfectly skilled to bring another into your world, a child who, for whatever reason, hasn't thrived in a traditional school setting.

Do you believe in the benefits of daily exercise? Check

into the amount of recess offered at your local schools, particularly low-income schools. What you find might shock you into action. Arm yourself with the data that shows the benefits of unstructured physical activity to struggling learners. Advocate for what is best for kids bearing the greatest amount of pressure with the fewest resources.

Do you want your kids to be devoted, lifelong readers? Volunteer to buddy up with a child who needs some extra help. Stock the school or classroom libraries.

Do you believe essential oils are a prime key for health and well-being? Research consistently shows that low-income families experience a higher rate of stress and illness. Find a way to transfer your knowledge and passion to a family in your neighborhood or town who could use support but struggles to put food on the table, much less Thieves oil on the feet.

Whatever your thing happens to be, make it your personal mission to carry that into the life of another child close to you. Start with one or a small handful. Mother them in whatever way serves them best—with your advocacy, your wisdom, your get-it-done-ness. Look at them with confidence and determination. Surprise them with the persistence of your presence. There are kids nearby whose lives would be improved by the warmth of your love and whose love, in return, would improve yours.

Yesterday, on the heels of a brutal weekend news cycle involving light and breezy topics such as white supremacy and the threat of nuclear war, I laced up my shoes and set out to start the week, as I always do.

My heart had been pounding for days, yet stepping out

into the air, greeting a fresh Monday along with my neighbors, I was reminded all over again that this is where it will have to begin. I cannot change the hearts of men. I am powerless to reroute the path of our country. I can chip away the barriers I see over time, and I should. But now is now, today is the day I've been given, and I want it to count. I want to believe that it can, that it is connected to the larger picture, and that, as one little neighborhood in Goshen, Indiana, moves toward a path of greater health and wholeness, so will the nation.

I did not set out to do anything spectacular, no grand gesture. (Mondays and grand gestures should be mutually exclusive.) All I did was greet the day. I showed up for my actual life, come what may. As usual, opportunity found me in my typical blend of bedhead and morning reluctance.

Here's how it all shook out.

Just as I was about to walk Ruby and Si to the elementary school, two middle schoolers showed up at our door. I handed them each a slice of banana bread on my way out and told them to have a great day. After school drop-off, I ran into my friend Dana at the crosswalk. The previous Friday, she'd told me through tears that she had been evicted from her home. Now, just a few days later, she shared the good news that she and her daughter had found a place up the street from ours. Walking home, I noticed wild patches of cornflowers in bloom along the curb, so I bent down to take a picture, grateful as ever that what some consider weeds others see as signs of life. A few houses down, my neighbor, Bubu, drove by and yelled his customary, "Good morning, sister!" out the window.

Next, I walked up to the middle school bus stop. I don't do this because I'm a helicopter mom, but because last year I caught on to the fact that large, unattended groups of middle school boys are a cautionary tale waiting to be written. Basically, I go to save them from themselves, Calvin included. Case in point: That very morning a young friend pulled a black ninja-style headband from his backpack, meaning no harm. "Dude, they'll call that gang paraphernalia so fast!" another boy said. Sadly, he was right. I opened my hand and, without a word, the neighborhood ninja dropped it in, laughing. "Daaaaang. You already finessed my beads last week and now you're finessing my headband!"

Their bus eventually came, and all I can say about that is, "Go with God, good middle school bus driver. You are a rose among loud, hormonal, Hot-Cheetos-for-breakfast-eating, lanyard-flipping thorns." When the bus pulled away and the dust cleared, I noticed three high schoolers looking a bit lost and forlorn and a middle schooler racing up the sidewalk. All of them had missed their bus and none of the four had alternate transportation. One was a complete stranger but gave her word that it was "fine" for her to accept a ride from me. I grabbed my keys and off we went, making the circuit from school to school. I was glad I had brushed my teeth.

My morning went differently than I had planned. It may have been slightly inconvenient. It took a bit of time, mostly because our neighborhood has long been landlocked by road construction the likes of which have caused lesser men and women to tear their clothes and lament humanity in the town square. It was also super easy, tremendously ordinary, and altogether my pleasure. I'd done nothing I wouldn't have done for my "own" kids. I have a hunch you'd do the same.

Last summer alone, my kids were mom-rescued a tidy handful of times after we suffered a few glaring parenting fails. In every case, another more-centered mom who maybe had done some yoga or drank some coffee or gotten an adequate night's rest swooped in to help, reserving judgment, focused only on the task at hand, to save the children.

We're moms. It's what we do.

The pundits may still be busy arguing in their neckties, tossing out anxiety-bombs and sweating through their collars. But over here in the neighborhood, the sun is shining and the weeds are the same blue as the sky. All of it is free, and that does something to me. This is the day to fling grace around like glitter, to pass out slices of banana bread, to tell the boys how handsome their ID pictures are, to help each other out and lift each other up. Let's open our homes and our passenger doors. Let's be sensitive and aware.

In the span of God's wide and rowdy family, we all belong to one another and there is no such thing as other people's children. Take a look around. Find someone to nurture. This is how we'll rise.

Chapter Fourteen

Arms Linked

Sometimes, the thing I miss most about my old life is the tranquility of my bird's-eye view. It's not the farmhouse of my dreams, the ample square footage, the sturdy salaries, or the sheen of success that I miss. It's being tucked in among the clouds where, if I even bothered looking down at all, the problems were antlike, no more than tiny smudges far below the comfort and beauty of the life I loved.

I miss the simplicity of my inward-facing world, wallpapered exclusively with the stuff I wanted and with myself. My family. My opinions. My faith. My security. I miss the luxury of a safe distance, where the only problems I worried about were my own. I was no more selfish then than I am today. I wasn't coldhearted. I just hadn't fallen from my perch. I didn't know what I didn't know. I hadn't acquired a taste for the complication of mixing my life into the lives around me, far different from my own.

The thing about paying attention to our ordinary places is that the more intently we study them, the more layered and detailed they become. Trouble surfaces, like the hidden images embedded in those old 3-D posters. Stare long enough, let your vision acclimate, and, *whoa*, there it is. It shows up inconveniently, shattering our easy answers. It rattles the gates of our tightly reined existence. It costs us the peace of oblivion and the consolation of our quiet esteem. Attentiveness isn't a life plan for living numb.

This is our warning. The more deeply our roots sink into the soil, the more we will uncover the places in our world where things aren't fair. We'll encounter different circumstances and be moved in different directions. We'll stop minding our own business in unique ways. But the question we're faced with will ring out in unison as we're pressed to decide whether we'll fight for those we love or close ranks and keep things tidy. *What are you going to do about this?*

God only knows the second option will likely feel safest. We'll want to run and hide, just as the Israelites wanted to do when they found themselves in an unfamiliar land. "Build homes, and plan to stay," he told them, through the prophet Jeremiah (29:5). Plant gardens. Create families.

Easy enough.

But then he goes too far, as he always does. He shakes us up and pokes into our personal space. "And work for the peace and prosperity of the city where I sent you into exile. Pray to the LORD for it, for its welfare will determine your welfare" (29:7).

Essentially, if those around us aren't free, then we aren't either.

This was a revelation I was contemplating when I first saw

Mack out my front windows, wandering aimlessly around the neighborhood. For all my early days spent waiting for God to give me something to do, when opportunity finally found me, I didn't feel ready. Swapping my binoculars for a chisel and shovel hinted at work more taxing than what I was hoping for.

But when Mack's situation came to my attention, I started chipping away, one stroke at a time, at the mystery behind his expulsion. What had appeared months earlier to be an impenetrable block of stone was revealing itself in excruciating detail. As I got to know him better, looking at the whites of his eyes, as my mom might say, the whole story emerged like a modern-day weeping, grieving Pietà.

Just like the oak trees dotting my path each day, the roots of the truth stretched disproportionately underground. Mack was barely five feet tall, still a little twitchy about making eye contact, and so soft-spoken that I often had to ask him to repeat himself. He was much too young to know the implications of the story being written for him by people doing their jobs without the aid of excavation.

The labels "troubled" and "dangerous" did not fit the kid standing on my porch, so I started digging. There was no margin for complacency. I knew what would likely follow for Mack. I'd seen it all in hindsight with our oldest son, Robert. I'd seen it in many of Cory's friends at the jail. Reality showed with blinding clarity that black boys are expelled far more frequently than others for identical offenses.[1] What tends to follow school expulsion is juvenile detention and, eventually, adult incarceration.

I had a preview of how Mack's life might play out if the world didn't begin to gaze on him with the same promise, expectation, and opportunity afforded other boys. This bright, funny, engaging child who had no serious history of major disciplinary trouble and who did not pose a threat to his community was pushed out of it and left alone.

Nell Bernstein, a researcher on race and education, said, "Children do best when they are held close."[2] I came to see that holding someone close can look very much like locking arms and demanding answers.

Tentatively at first, taking great care not to back myself into a corner, bite off more than I could chew, or suffer the consequences of any relevant idioms, I started asking questions. Tossed out of middle school for the entire year, there were no services in place for him—no alternative programming, no tutoring, no second chances.

Without meaning to, certainly without hoping to, I'd found a crack in the very public school system I champion, along with a reminder that constructive critique is good and necessary, even and especially when it's personal. I had two choices: retreat or engage. I love and tirelessly support our public school system, but I love the people it serves more. People > Systems. Every time. Standing with the individual might stretch our ideas about time management and overall ROI, but this is often how broken systems begin to be repaired. It can be difficult sometimes to discern fracture in the context of thousands of people, but one child rises up as living proof, grabbing our attention and refusing to let go. As the singular illuminates the whole, we are left to move either toward or away from the trouble at hand.

Sister Helen Prejean said, "Being kind in an unjust system is not enough."[3] Was I ready to heave a portion of Mack's burden onto my own shoulders, even if it caused a fuss and many wouldn't understand?

I stewed and lost some sleep. I checked my motives and fretted over my reputation. Finally, I wrote one e-mail, a single domino that tipped a hundred more.

Many phone calls, correspondences, crying jags, boatloads of meetings (some in administrative offices and some on my front lawn) later, on the heels of a good deal of hand-wringing, working closely with his mom, and exhausting all other options, it was decided that Mack would come sit with me at my kitchen table for tutoring each weekday from one to three in the afternoon.

For many of you, this sounds like a dream scenario. I, on the other hand, am cut from a different cloth. I shower my kids' teachers with support and encouragement because I am in awe of the work they do and I want them to keep doing it so I never have to. I was the only girl in elementary school who didn't harbor some future teacher goals.

What I'm saying is, as we inspect our geography for wounds, we aren't given the luxury of choosing what we'll uncover or our role in delivering first aid.

I thought my job was to notice the problem and connect the right people. I honestly believed (foolishly, arrogantly) that I would convince the school to change their tune. When it became evident that this might, at least for a while, fall on me, I was more bummed out than invigorated and grateful.

"What are you going to do about this?" I asked God on repeat. To my great frustration, his response every time was, "How much bread do you have?"

I told him I didn't have time. This wasn't in my skill set. Mack deserved better.

Quite plainly, he was unmoved by my laundry list of excuses.

Time was passing, and Mack was floundering. They said he could return the following school year, but what would that look like for an eighth grader with a target on his back who'd been on a year-long hiatus from learning?

How much bread do you have?

Honestly, I didn't have much, and what I did have wasn't the good kind of bread. With great hesitation, I held out my slice and a half of bad bread. Wasting no time, God snatched them up, making a feast of scraps.

To break the ice on our first day I asked the shy guy staring at my dirty floor a question. "Who is Mack?"

"A kid who makes a lot of mistakes," he answered.

The narrative was taking root. It doesn't take long.

We got to work watching YouTube videos on the travails of seventh-grade math. On more than one occasion I corrected his work, only to find out he had been right all along. Math! It's the worst.

We read *The Outsiders*, along with short stories and poems by Langston Hughes. When there was time, we'd move to the living room, and I'd read a chapter of *Tuck Everlasting* aloud. We put our noses to the stone, but we had some fun. On our drive to the Boys & Girls club each day, I mothered him, nosing into his business, while he manned the radio and sang along.

We were comrades, woven into the new normal of the other's life. But as the end of the year barreled toward us, my numerical deficiencies still worried me. I was constantly concerned that we were creating a false sense of security, that our hard work wasn't nearly enough to bridge the chasm he'd been pushed into.

Cory carried our concerns off to his weekly lunch meeting with a group of ragtag former pastors, and they stepped into formation, offering advice and tangible help, helping me shuttle him around when I couldn't.

One of them also connected us with a retired high school English teacher. The day we met, she interrupted my planned dissertation on Mack and his many glowing attributes. "I'm ready to get started. I don't need to know anything else about him. I've kept my schedule open since retiring, knowing God would bring along the right opportunity. I don't need to think it over. This is it." (Do you think this made me weepy? You know me so well.)

Though math was still woefully within my jurisdiction, every Tuesday and Thursday thereafter I gratefully passed Mack off to an expert equipped to disciple him in the ways of grammar and reading comprehension.

Another influential member of our community showed up at my door unexpectedly soon after. He ended our conversation with this, "If we would just all do the one thing we're wired to do, the world would be a different place for our neighbors." The second he walked out the door I scrambled for a pen and wrote it down. Days later, thanks in part to a man who had never even met Mack, the school contacted me to say they had a new system in place to better meet the needs of students like him. Finally, together, we were getting somewhere.

When I was a kid, my church had a prayer-chain system in place in which urgent concerns were strung from telephone line to telephone line into a safety net of unquestionable caring. I will never discount the power of prayer, but pairing it with physical action is infinitely better. I was bearing witness to the church in action, lifting up one of its own and carrying him to safety.

It's true that it takes a village to raise a child, but it goes both ways. Sometimes, it takes a child to raise up a village, shining light on its shared purpose to work for the sake of each other.

———

In the book of Joshua we read a dramatic tale of conquests, spies, an out-of-the-way inn, and the woman inside, Rahab, who chose to meddle in the affairs of Joshua's two undercover agents, hiding them from the king of Jericho at the risk of her own peril. She had her reasons for getting involved. But above all, she believed in the power of the Lord, who "made a dry path" through the sea for the Israelites (Josh. 2:10). Adequately terrified by the magnitude of such power, she determined to stay on the right side of it. You might say Rahab had a robust fear of the Lord. So, with a clear view of what was at stake, she chose to stand against the regime and with those God stood with.

I imagine she didn't feel peace about this plan to collude with spies who sought to destroy her people. I'm guessing she was a ball of jangled nerves, experiencing anxiety-related bathroom issues and second-guessing herself. At any rate, she struck the deal and held up her end of it, hanging a scarlet thread from her window as the terms dictated.

Most Bible translations refer to Rahab as a prostitute or harlot. Others make a case that this label is unfair. I personally think it's enough to call her a human, doing her best in spite of the hardships and occasionally leaving a trail of wreckage. Isn't that all of us? God stationed Rahab in Jericho for a reason, with specific work to do. The same is true for me and you.

The day will never arrive that I am not astonished by God's eagerness to carry out his plans through the likes of us. His methodology for getting things done is a head-scratcher for the ages. With us by his side, everything is guaranteed to take one thousand times longer along a path potholed with our mess-ups and general antics. It would be so much more efficient to just do it all himself while we were napping or something.

He doesn't tire of us. He doesn't write us out of the script or make rash decisions about our fate. He hitches his glory to our ruin and keeps on trucking, delighted by every tiny step we make in the right direction. When Calvin was a baby, he was hesitant and fearful about the task of walking. He cruised around the coffee table for months on end, all hands on deck. Now and then, though, he'd feel a surge of bravery, pulling his hands off the tabletop and throwing them into the air for no more than one second. Every time, we lost our minds cheering. We thought he was the bravest baby we'd ever imagined. I picture God like that with us.

Taping that image of God's love to my mirror, how could I see anyone as beneath *my* enthusiastic optimism and abiding support?

Centuries after Joshua conquered Jericho with Rahab's help, James would point back to her as a reminder that "just as the body is dead without breath, so also faith is dead without good works" (James 2:26). Rahab, an ordinary woman with a complicated story of her own, ended up forming part of the lineage of King Jesus. His is a family tree shaped entirely of common people, which is to say hot messes, epic failures, the disaster-prone, the chronic foot-in-mouthers, the surly, the cynical, the greedy, the short-fused, the undisciplined, the smack-talkers, the arrogant, the passive-aggressors, the codependent, and the ones who are incapable of taking their socks off without turning them into an inside-out ball of overripe foot odor. True, we have our upsides. But we're also sort of the worst. Persistently I neglect to love God with my whole heart, yet his eye remains glued to this sparrow. He's right here, out on a limb with us when he could have just watched us from the sky.

———

Our eyes were conditioned for dimly lit places. Waking up to what's happening around us and choosing to step into it will be uncomfortable, maybe forever. It will be unpopular, maybe forever. But it will move inside us, this awakening, at the speed of biology. Cells dividing, truth conquering lies, overcoming what must die in its place.

The good news is that Jesus waits for us somewhere in the trenches, in the skin and hair and unfamiliar scent of wanting. He's already there in the thick of it, and should we decide other people are not our problem, we owe it to ourselves to acknowledge that we're trading our perceived safety and comfort for an encounter with the holy God who continues to hold us close despite our own versions of expulsion notices, rap sheets, and handcuffs.

It's a new year. Mack is back in school as an eighth grader. You should have seen the pride on his mom's face at the glowing reports of his teachers at conferences. "He's funny!" "He's engaged!" "He's got a knack for math!" We weren't a bit surprised. Still, the road feels rocky. For an eighth-grade boy unfairly labeled high risk, the constant scrutiny is a storm cloud just overhead. Not a day goes by that I don't smell rain.

I don't miss him at my kitchen table, but that's only because he's become one of Calvin's best friends, in our home often, rapping and dancing in the basement, eating hot dogs, Hot Cheetos, and hot wings with my kids. This Christmas, he joined us on stage at church and read his Advent lines with dignity and courage. "Stay gold," he says sometimes as he's leaving, a reference to Ponyboy Curtis and our time spent with him under last winter's bleached-out sky.

This is my prayer, that as we look around and locate pain, widening our scope when necessary, we'll have the guts to take swift action. I pray that we'll all go down together, arms linked, hoarse from shouting on behalf of those found at the short end of justice. I pray that down at street level, we'll feel the tremor of God's power and decide, once and for all, that our feet were made for low places and worthy battles. We'll hang a scarlet cord from the window as our promise to keep meddling for the sake of the kingdom.

Chapter Fifteen

Redefining Success

A couple of years into living in our neighborhood, Cory and I spontaneously decided to host a free family photo day. I'm not sure what inspired us other than two simple realities: (1) Cory takes pretty pictures, and (2) many of our neighbors might not have the opportunity to do this small thing we take for granted.

After the initial idea sparked, we talked it to death, then got to work trying to micromanage every single detail and account for every possible pitfall in advance, believing if everything was exactly right, the odds for success would bend in our favor. It was precisely this fixation on perfection and the fear of failure that prompted us to call the whole thing off before we'd even gotten it off the ground.

Still, we couldn't outrun the idea so, the following year, we tried again. In the time that had lapsed, we had learned more about the rhythms of our place. Our old assumptions about how God worked and who he blessed were being replaced with healthier ones. We were learning to do the next right thing, walking in obedience in this place we loved with no guarantees of the outcomes we hoped for. That October, *this* was the next right thing. Maybe the weather would mess with us. Maybe no one would trust us enough. Maybe, maybe, maybe.

Cory put together a basic, bilingual flyer, and he and the kids walked fifty of them door to door. (I drummed up a logical reason to be unavailable because this step hit all my introvert trigger points.)

It was impossible to gauge interest. Some of the neighbors had been more than a little wary. Many, due to a language barrier, were unable to communicate directly with Cory. And though it was entirely free, we knew the skeptics would be doubtful. But we forged on.

The day before our planned event was a picture-perfect October day. Brilliant skies, maple trees thick with leaves the color of sunsets and tangerines. Things were looking up.

The next morning, Saturday, we woke to gray skies and a twenty-degree temperature drop. As the rain fell, we turned to each other and shrugged. We had done our imperfect part. We knew it was all right if our day was a flop. But a few embers from my success-warped theology still burned in my belly. I still had a hunch God would "show up in a big way," as so many in my past might have promised.

When the time came for our photo day event, the rain slowed a bit, as if on cue. It was still pretty chilly, and yesterday's magical leaves were now in sodden, brown piles at our feet, but we consoled ourselves that the light was always better on a cloudy day. Cory framed his shot, then we hopped back in the van to warm up while we waited, the windshield wipers mocking us. *Uh-uh. Nope.*

No one came.

After a while, I drove home with the kids, fielding questions from the back-seaters. "Why did we keep waiting there?" "Why didn't anyone come?" "Why did Daddy stay?"

I told them what was just beginning to bloom in me: obedience is worth the risk of failure. Between their questions, I spun through an entire reel of self-talk, reminding myself that my life, my days, my DSLR camera are not my own.

And then.

My phone buzzed with a text from Cory.

"A family just showed up!"

I turned the van around.

There they were, two parents. Eight kids. A mash-up of bloodlines and heartstrings and *you-belong-to-me*s. These were people who knew a thing or two about what makes a family. In puffy coats and matching *nothing*, they squeezed close and smiled.

"We planned all week for this!"

"We've never had a family picture."

"We switched weekends with their mom so we could all be together."

I cried the whole way home when it was over. We had been so close to a different ending, one where they planned all week and zipped their coats, then showed up at an empty park.

If we had known how it would go down, that only one family would show up, I'm almost certain we wouldn't have gone to the trouble. It probably wouldn't have seemed worth it.

Was the day a failure? Or was it a success?

Several years ago, a book was published on what had been a little-known passage in the Old Testament book of 1 Chronicles. *The Prayer of Jabez: Breaking Through to the Blessed Life* took the world by storm, particularly the Western world. It was based on two little lines of scripture: "'Oh, that you would bless me and expand my territory! Please be with me in all that I do, and keep me from all trouble and pain!' And God granted him his request" (1 Chron. 4:10).

People lined up to claim its promises. An assurance of more, more, more? Sign us up.

The book also had a fair share of critics, but, drumroll, please: the numbers spoke for themselves. It was an unequivocal bestseller.

As a nation, it turns out we quite liked a God who gave good gifts. We adored the ideas of avoiding trouble and gaining influence and power. As we're prone to do, we noodled scripture to fit our modernized worldview, then stood back, admiring this vision of a vast estate, vowing to use all God gave for his glory and fame.

Sure, we would.

Not surprisingly, the author of the book wasn't the first preacher to stumble on those Old Testament lines. Charles Spurgeon, the Baptist "Prince of Preachers" in nineteenth-century England, wrote this about Jabez's prayer: "To a great extent we find that we must sow in tears before we can reap in joy. . . . You may expect a blessing in serving God if you are enabled to persevere under many discouragements."[1] From his view, God's blessing was centered around our service, and it would come with a heap of sorrow.

Bigger and greater was never the point at all. The promise was the fruit of endurance.

The past five years in my family's life have been a long loop of discovering how perilously incompatible kingdom success and cultural success really are.

I spent my first decade and a half pining for status. I climbed ladders, bolting to a better job whenever the opportunity presented itself. I worked insane hours. Once, when I had a job in sales, my manager referred to me as a shark, and I beamed, unsure if I'd ever received a greater compliment. Early in our marriage, Cory and I moved to Washington, DC, and took entry-level jobs on Capitol Hill. In the evenings I slipped into my walking shoes for the commute home, listening in on conversations between glossy women impeccably dressed in muted tones.

I pretended to judge the logo-obsessed, materialistic, success-driven culture we were immersed in, but, in reality, I wanted it. I wanted the tailored suits, the salary, the Saturday brunches in Georgetown. I sure as heck wanted the Louis Vuitton bag roughly the size of a hybrid car hanging from my shoulder.

Two promotions later, we were back in Indiana, living in the farmhouse of our dreams. The particular things I wanted had shifted, but, stripped down, they were exactly the same. I wanted to be seen as a good, Christian woman, financially stable and then some. I wanted family photos every year where my adorable kids were dressed like crewcuts models and smiled directly into the camera. I wanted safety. Security. I wanted that toned-down, polite, midwestern version of success.

We worked and schemed, daydreaming expansions for a house that was already more than we needed and a flashier SUV. *Someday.* We took what we wanted and said it was from God, borrowing a manhandled theology from the Christian culture at large, where church success is measured by "nickels and noses" and where it's always a race to be right.

There's something so cozy about the sheen of success. Drive a certain car, live in a certain kind of home in the right zip code. Send your kids to the best school you can find. Buy the right toys, vacation twice a year, wear the right jeans, the right eye cream, the latest edition of the cutest boot. This is how we pretend to hold it together. This is how we do it.

When the hangers I'd draped my worth on finally snapped, I felt exposed. Our values had shifted away from the bootstrap theology that wrongly says God helps those who help themselves. Cory and I were suddenly aware of what a sham our efforts had been. We found ourselves drawn to small and forgotten places, but in order to get there, we first had to smell the stench of a gossip mill in overdrive at our expense, grinding our reputation into dust. Beneath that millstone I began to understand just how guilty—politely, quietly, yet truly guilty—I had been of scrutinizing myself and others according to the very metrics God despises.

For as long as man has existed, God has spent most of his time extracting us from the clouds of our pride and setting us back in place. Whether we like it or not, our feet were made to get dirty. Down here at ground level, we have no choice but to deeply feel our need for him.

I know this to be true, but for me it was still complicated.

After the dust settled on this new chapter, after all we had learned about choosing low places, I began to slip back into my old ways, equating purpose with success and success with gains. I was constantly tempted to quantify every little thing we were doing. The difference was, what we were doing now was thoroughly enmeshed with our everyday living. This was no ministry that met once a week. It wasn't a job we could clock out of at the end of the day. It was our actual life, hidden in Christ.

Such a lovely thing to muck up, but we did it anyway. I spent my days doing first-grade math. I counted warm bodies in the pews, the number of neighbors I knew by name, the months of sobriety for various friends, even the number of kids at the bus stop. I did my best to shove the expansive kingdom into the pinhole frame of this unsatisfied world. No surprise, it didn't fit.

Along the way, it became impossible to ignore the dreaded rumble of truth: I was still terrified of being ordinary. I had let myself believe for a minute that I'd risen above this basic curse of humankind. Nope. I was here in my overstuffed house trying to fit into last year's yoga pants and still horribly afraid of living an unspectacular life. Though my definition of *special* may have been whacked around beyond recognition in recent years, I was still quite happy to wear the crown, even if (especially if?) the world around me found it a bit misshapen and dull.

I craved validation from all of those who had doubted our choices. Part of me still warmed to the classic martyr-lite complex, where I imagined God just a bit prouder of me for my sacrifice and utility. More than anything, I wanted to see lives swept up into the goodness of Jesus. I wanted to watch this place I love flourish. I couldn't help but want a tiny slice of the credit. "People aren't projects," I insisted. But if that was true, why was I still posing as a social scientist, spinning theories and calculating results? This exposed my pride in innumerable ways. It also stripped me of the joy of small victories.

Here's what we've been slowly learning. Success is faithfulness. *Our* faithfulness. It's a conclusion that can only be drawn as we put the theory to work, and let me tell you, the work is agonizing at times. It's hard to remain committed to the growth quietly germinating underground. In a world that prizes production quality and happy endings, it can be painful to watch life play out like a melancholy indie flick.

When it comes to loving and working for the good of our places, there is no other way. To obsess over positive outcomes is to miss the low simmer of redemption. The temptation to measure our effectiveness by the world's standards causes us to prematurely declare defeat or success. It tempts us to only engage with people we feel will make us look good, plotting our interactions, our entanglements, our *friends*.

In trying to avoid the mess, we would also miss the magic

of looking closely at the life we're in, choosing lifeblood over sterile analysis and sticking around for as long as it takes.

For Cory and the devoted volunteers at the jail, success means welcoming their incarcerated friends back time after time with open arms, reserving judgment and self-righteousness and allowing space for the exquisite work of God, unrushed and right on time.

For me, success means believing this year will be better for my struggling kiddo. It also means that I'll keep making lunch on Sundays, never knowing who might show up, not derailed by worries that it will be for nothing.

For some of the people I love, success might mean avoiding the needle three days out of five and coming clean when they've messed up. It's a start, so we celebrate it.

Sometimes success means reconciling. It means telling the hardest truth. It means getting locked up again, and receiving it as a gift.

The kingdom of God defines *success* as the intangible, unmistakable ability to cling to hope when everyone else is wagging their fingers and shaking their heads.

In these years of discovery, it's becoming clear that the smaller my world and my work become, the more grounded I am in God's vast kingdom. Here, where our home, our school, our church, many of our friends, and most of our community involvement exist within a few blocks, we are active, attentive participants in the unfolding of God's story for us as a collective.

I know this is the exception. Most of us deal with long

commutes and schools across town. Some of us don't even *see* another human within a mile. If I paint the tight borders of my place in a way that's overly idyllic, it's only because I'm smitten with it. That's all. I know it's not practical or even feasible for most of us. Trust me, that's okay. It's not about numbers. There's no mile marker and no city limit that can separate you from the dazzling plan of God.

We look into the place God has put us, "awed to heaven, rooted in earth" as Brueggemann would say; we discover the way of faithfulness.[2]

That is success.

My friend and neighbor, Bubu, is one of the wisest men I know. I have to refrain from including him in every chapter I write. Not long ago, on one of our Monday night treks through Matthew, he shared his thoughts on chapter 21 verse 21, where Jesus basically tells us that if we believe, we can hurl Mt. Mitchell into the Atlantic.

I cringed even reading it, so egregiously have I seen this passage abused throughout my life, sometimes at my own hands. But I've learned to straighten up in my chair when Bubu speaks.

"When I moved to this neighborhood, I remembered this verse often," he said. "I thought my job was to go around and make sure all of my neighbors came to know God. This was my mountain. Over time, I lost my intensity with this. People kept moving away, and I wasn't really seeing any results. Now I am wondering if the miracle Jesus is calling down is for me to stay here and keep loving my neighbor, little by little inviting them into the family of God. The mountain isn't my neighbors. The mountain is me."

Paul Sparks from Parish Collective, coauthor of *The New Parish: How Neighborhood Churches are Transforming Mission, Discipleship, and Community,* said it so well in what he called the "Reverse Prayer of Jabez": "God, shrink our territory, and narrow our boundaries, that we might truly be a blessing to all."[3]

Here, where God's kingdom is moving closer to where we stand, down is the destination, small is great, and invisible lights the way.

Part Four

Love Song for the Long Haul

Chapter Sixteen

A Theology of Endurance

It was the year 2000, a new millennium. I was driving through an unfamiliar side of town trying to decode the directions I'd scribbled on the back of an envelope, on my way to an interview for my first real job. In the weeks leading up to that moment I'd done all the necessary prep for this important mile marker on my journey to actual adulthood. I sat in the apartment where Cory and I had lived since our wedding a year or so prior and dialed up J.Crew on the landline to order a proper business suit. There would be no boring black for this savvy woman on the cusp of a career in sales. No, I went for the silvery-blue-gray wool crepe, certain it was a classic that would stand the test of time. My days spent stocking and folding the denim wall at Gap had almost come to an end. I had my hair trimmed at a strip mall. I lined my lips with my favorite eyeliner (this was a thing in my life for a while. Forgive me, Lord), filled them in with Dr. Pepper chapstick, and was on my way, armed with the college degree I had never used. I zipped through the city, checking my makeup at red lights, taking cleansing breaths to try to quiet the butterflies flapping in my gut. I was headed toward a better life. I was ready.

It's all fine and good, as they say, until you forget you're driving on a one-way street and you turn directly in front of two lanes of traffic, instantly pummeled on your driver's side by a cargo van on a mission.

The crash spun my crumpled Pontiac Sunfire a full 180, landing me right by the front door of my would-be employer. Emotionally whiplashed into a curious place of calm, I sat in my paradoxically pastel business suit while neck-tied strangers picked glass from my hair and dabbed hydrogen peroxide on the cuts along my hands and cheek.

A panicked desperation to reach Cory washed over me, off working a construction job hours away, unreachable. All I wanted in that moment was to teleport to our basement apartment, lay my head on his lap, and sob my ever-living guts out. I wanted to burn that bad omen suit and pretend the whole thing had never happened.

Instead, I shoved my true feelings to a far corner and sat through the interview as planned. I fought my base impulse knowing it would serve me well. I was good at self-control. Or so I thought. When the human resources director asked about my biggest weakness, I fluently delivered the cliché go-tos: that I can be a perfectionist, that I sometimes expect too much of myself and others, that I'm competitive to a fault. I was unshakable. From my peripheral vision, I saw a tow truck hoist my beloved car, now totaled, onto its flatbed and haul it away. I didn't turn my head. I didn't even flinch.

Cory picked up pizza on his way home and spent the evening kissing my forehead and telling me how worried he had been when the call had come in.

Two days later, they offered me the job.

We were still there in that drab apartment when our marriage crumbled six months later. It happened fast, like steel meeting glass. And it happened in slow motion, a car veering into the wrong lane under the watchful eye of no one in particular.

———

I have always thought of myself as a leaver.

When I was four, I began the long tradition of spending part of each summer with my aunt, uncle, and cousin in Pennsylvania. I fell into step, blending seamlessly into their routine. They bought my pass to the community pool, noticed when my pants became high-waters, doled out my allowance, and took me on lavish family vacations to places like Disney World and Niagara Falls. For one month of the year, I lived as the fraternal twin of my cousin, Vickie. I went to Catholic Vacation Bible School, watched Billy Idol on MTV, and developed a taste for fried pierogies and freedom.

I was marked as a girl who went places, my connections sewn with elastic. I always went home to the old Ohio farmhouse and the family inside it, but I could stretch just as easily as I could dream. Brave and sturdy, I assimilated quickly. I missed curfew often. I went to college out of state and married a Hoosier. I moved. I changed my mind. I drove too fast.

When the dust of our marital collapse settled, it was second nature for me to want to run. The fight-or-flight response, hardwired deeply within our physiology, is considered one of mankind's most primal urges. Heap stress on us, make us believe survival is shaky, and hormones flood our central nervous system, instinctively diverting our behavior into one of two outcomes. Here's what one expert wrote:

> By its very nature, the fight or flight system bypasses our rational mind—where our more well thought out beliefs exist—and moves us into "attack" mode. This state of alert causes us to perceive almost everything in our world as a possible threat to our survival. . . . Fear becomes the lens through which we see the world. . . . Our heart is not open. Our rational mind is disengaged. Our consciousness is focused on fear, not love.[1]

A collision of trust and secrets had left us shattered, with no one but each other to tend to the nicks and gashes. Left alone long enough, anguish can fade to apathy, and I'm still not sure which is more dangerous. We circled each there in apartment 4D, still cooking dinner, still paying the bills. We'd lost our fight to the fire, so we sat at opposite ends of the couch and watched David Letterman. At times we still laughed together. Those were the nights I would cry when I went to bed. I knew I would miss him, but I also knew it was over. Lapsing into deeply interior lives, we told no one what was happening. Divorce was not an option, both of us had been warned early on, and the inevitable shame of the church loomed large. On the darkest nights, I wished the cargo van had hit me harder.

And then, right in the middle of the guilt and uncertainty, a miracle.

I was walking past the mirror I had painted blue to match our wedding towels. Catching my reflection, wrecked, ruined, and depleted of hope, I was struck with a thought as clear as the blue eyes of the husband I'd been avoiding. The words were inaudible and entirely inescapable: *Do you see how hard the enemy is fighting to destroy your marriage? Just imagine the plans I have for you, together.*

Isn't it just like God to show up uninvited and derail our plans for self-loathing? Silently, the seed took root. Maybe, despite what I was feeling in the rawness of my present life, I could be a stayer. Maybe, the Jesus I loved could be the Jesus I trusted in the face of impossible odds. The healing didn't happen in my heart, not at first. It landed bluntly in my hypothalamus. I was still sunk in incomprehensible emotional distress, but my old circuitry had been yanked out, new wiring grafted in somewhere amid the sadness of ordinary life. Finally, I unearthed the faith to believe that I could shelve my escape plans and choose to start over, a fighter.

The years ticked by and our hearts healed, one mercy at a time. We returned to our frailty and apologized more often. We got better at telling the truth. We held on with a white-knuckle grip, even when it seemed easier not to. The low times dwindled, fewer and further between, and when doubt banged at our door, we now knew we didn't have to welcome it in and make a bed for it.

We started a family. We grew. We fell in love for the long haul. Eventually, to our great surprise, we adapted to city life and all that came with it. Our lives took on the air of adventure, pulling us tightly toward each other and a new rush of uncharted land.

Though our marriage was stronger than ever, having assimilated to the practice of leaving, moving on, and conquering the unknown, I grew antsy and bored. Staring straight through the life I truly loved, I strained to find bigger cities and grittier neighborhoods. At night I dreamed of running down unfamiliar streets, snapping awake sweaty and buzzed from the rush of imagined endorphins. It was all coming back to me.

I did not want to slow down. I was addicted to upheaval.

This unrest bled fluidly into the corners of my life. Once wonderstruck by our bright reality, I now entertained fantasies about the larger house one street over that was begging for a renovation. Conditioned to view leaving as a viable option the instant something didn't meet my expectations, I was particularly fleet of foot when it came to our church, which, after two years of early bliss, was now effectively splitting before our eyes.

Week in, week out, we were at the mercy of an ecclesial roller-coaster bound for imminent derailment. We got to work steadily wearing down the interest of our long-suffering friends, growing tired of our own voices along the way. Most began to gently suggest that perhaps rather than languishing in this spiritual stall pattern and disintegrating into two more bitter pew-warmers, we might simply find another church home. It happened all the time. To most of us, church was faithfulness spun through a revolving door. Divorcing a particular congregation was as common as a Sunday potluck. If you didn't happen to enjoy what was being served, you simply saw yourself out. It wasn't the end of the world.

But for the first time, we found that our impulse to cut bait and run wasn't that simple. Without realizing it, our hearts had been won over to a parish framework, where a church and its place are fundamentally intertwined, one wrapping around and through the other as they tend to the needs of their people across generations. Needlessly headstrong and profoundly frustrated, we felt both abandoned and entitled, so leaving seemed like the logical conclusion. And yet, this church was itself our neighbor.

It was time for us to course-correct, past blind fighting and toward an enduring posture of staying. We became devoted students to the school of stubborn hope. Releasing ourselves and each other from the chains of stature and size, we got reacquainted with God, who saw entire worlds in water and earth and found delight in the small, the plain, and the utterly dependent. At last, we stopped obsessing about whether or not we had reached the limits of our grace for our church and began focusing instead on our own infirmity and our personal contributions to the pain.

We chose to stay and fight.

As always, the winds of the Spirit were waiting to astound us. The once-empty pews filled. Men and women paying their debts and living at the mercy of a crushing system were greeted by seasoned grandmas who memorized their names in no time flat. Just last Sunday I witnessed an encounter between Len, a young man enthusiastically embracing his fresh start, and Arlene, a woman in her eighties with no official children of her own. After she greeted him by name (she knows everyone while the rest of us struggle to keep up), he grinned at her. "Arlene, you got your hair cut, didn't you?"

She patted the top of her head shyly. "I needed one!"

"Well," he replied, "you look beautiful."

My church family and the anatomy of our time together has reshaped my view of Sunday services. We come to worship, to grow into one another and toward the hope of our salvation. But I'm no longer interested in critiquing the particulars of the sermon or nit-picking the song choice. Now I see the physical togetherness we share as vital. Over time, this is what forms a loose band of acquaintances into family. We pass the peace, crossing the sanctuary to hug our new friends and invite them to lunch. They bring their girlfriends, their stepkids, their babies dressed to the nines. At sharing time, we hand them the mic, and they gain, for maybe the first time, a voice among a body of believers who vows to support and love them, come what may.

Week after week, each of us experiences the spark of being loved and chosen by someone who the world might say wasn't meant for us. They came to us entirely unable to fix our financial deficits or alleviate our need for human people to do things like take out the trash, teach classes, and flip the occasional pancake. They kept showing up in the same jeans they wore to their factory jobs and began healing us in ways that were both harder to detect and infinitely more vital.

God uses the willing hearts of his imperfect body to turn us back to him. This is one of his signature moves.

————

Almost twenty years since the near decimation of my marriage, I have remembered that moment by the mirror in our tiny apartment one thousand times, minimum. I remembered it at the therapist's office, in the U-Haul driving east, in the overpriced DC apartment with the parquet floor. I remembered it at the Detroit airport, when a stranger handed me a four-month-old Calvin and he stared into my eyes like I was exactly who he was looking for. I remembered it in the delivery room where another woman labored Ruby into the world and again in Seoul, South Korea, when Silas cried until he surrendered to sleep in my arms.

I remembered it on our first night in the city and during my first visit to the jail. I remembered it when Robert and his friends sat laughing and hoarding all the Wi-Fi at my kitchen island, and after every bad dream, when I instinctively curve my shape around my sleeping husband—my safest place—as a reminder of what is real.

Sometimes God splits the seas. Other times, he pulls what

has been split back together, and stitches it up. Any scars are a reminder that what the world calls dead is often alive underground, saving its show-stopper blooms for the ones who stuck around.

Two years after we sat on the cliff edge of a church that was left waiting for her own death, I have found a place where my spirit finds sanctuary. The young men, old women, and rowdy kids are the essence of who I am, stripped of all my props. Some of us are marked with cheap tattoos, others with quiet privilege. Some of us wear sensible sweater sets, and others wear leather and chains. We all have been welcomed as the sojourner, no longer bound by shame, but set free by the rescue of God's incomparable, unexpected grace. We all have felt the embrace of a frail body defying its own death—*You came to us. Please, don't leave.*

Now, there's no way around our limitations, our "sufficient depravity," as Dallas Willard said.[2] We believe again that a God who paid special attention to mustard seeds, water, bread, children, birds, and mud finds delight in the small and ordinary. Fully human, adequately broken, we know any credit isn't ours, growing more patient with each other as we go, forgiving as we are forgiven. It doesn't matter which hymn we're singing on a given Sunday. My song is always the same: "I almost missed this. I almost missed this."

In the book of Jeremiah God called the Israelites out for caving to their base fears. Wayward and weary, they were stuck in a stall pattern where trusting God was tough and running back to their perceived idea of safety seemed to make the most sense. "If you are determined to go to Egypt and live there," he warned, "the very war and famine you fear will catch up to you, and you will die there" (42:15–16). "Stay here in this land. If you do, I will build you up and not tear you down; I will plant you and not uproot you" (v. 10).

Choosing to stay, at times, can be unhealthy or even impossible. Other times, it is obedient surrender, and we just have to stick it out until the good stuff begins. Oh, Lord, remind us that what we really want is more of you. You show us what it means to remain where you have placed us with great purpose—in the rumble of the city, down a winding lane, in the cookie-cutter 'burbs where pain might show up in less obvious ways, but is breathing hot down our necks all the same.

Show us the real way of worship, and grant us the guts to belong to each other when it's hardest. Teach us to walk in place, memorizing the lay of this unimpressive land and calling it good. Help us to hang on for the encore, where your best work often waits.

Prone to wander, Lord, we feel it.

But you are here, staring back at us in every face and every scar. You keep talking to us when we don't want to listen. You remind us that you came to be with us, and even when it seemed like you left, you didn't.

You are here, tuning our hearts to endurance, teaching us a love song for the long haul.

Help us to endure when we feel dog-tired.

Have your way.

Chapter Seventeen

The Discipleship
of Sticking Around

After we adopted Robert nearly five years ago, moving him into what forevermore shall be Robert's room in our basement, there was a short but ready line of people waiting to warn us about all that might go wrong. Concern was raised over the little kids' safety, my safety, and the general foolishness of claiming a nineteen-year-old with a felony as our own.

We were dauntless.

Looking back, there has been infighting, outfighting, and plenty of late-night kitchen fighting. Yet though we are no strangers to blame, guilt, ridiculously unfair expectations, outlandish entitlements (all mine), unexplained mood swings, minor setbacks, and monstrous pitfalls, our certainty has never been overrun with doubt. Yes, we have all had to take a crowbar to our forecast for the future a time or two, but not once, under the cover of even the darkest night, have we harbored a crumb of regret. We give each other the blues sometimes, sure.

But we are among one another's greatest adventures, with each other to the blistering, brilliant end.

"But are you discipling him?" some have asked. I'll admit, on the other side of my pride, their question had me wondering. I was brought up thinking discipleship had to involve a workbook, a highlighter, and an accountability partner. By that definition, *no*, we weren't discipling Robert, or anyone for that matter. But were we doing enough? More often than not, my daily quiet time consists of walking in my neighborhood, caramelizing onions, and chasing the moon. Who am I to be trusted with such fragile work?

———

I was sitting at the kitchen table working one afternoon when a commotion tore through the quiet. Two frustrated parents walked down the sidewalk, trying to get where they were going, when one of their little kids suddenly realized, with alarming urgency, that he indeed *did* have to go potty. It couldn't possibly have escaped my attention.

Hard at work writing my first book, *Falling Free*, the process was systematically stripping me of everything I thought I knew about writing. On top of that slight speedbump, I also lacked a solid grasp on the very life I was writing about—the shaky peril we seemed to be slumping toward or the perplexing gratification it brought us. All I knew was that I was hungry to get to know the people near me, and for an introvert with deep mind-my-own-business tendencies, this vast, instinctive departure from my personality was proof of God. So at least there was that.

When the young family passed by, it might as well have been Jesus himself standing with his mouth pressed against the window screen. *Hello? Can you hear me?* Riddled with self-doubt as always (should I just mind my own business?), I opened the door and invited these perfect strangers into my bathroom, which is to say, into my life. We didn't trade names or numbers. The whole event felt pretty inconsequential.

Two years later, I was passing the peace with everyone else at church when a woman approached, wrapping me in a hug while I scrambled to figure out who she was and why she seemed to know me. "I'm Heather! We used your bathroom that one time!" She pointed to a blond-haired toddler clutching her leg. "This is Matthew, the baby I was holding that day."

Just like that, she was back, like so many other Heathers who show up, wander off, and circle around again when we least expect it. We're still here, right where they left us. They're boomerangs, bearing the image of God. It always feels excessively lucky, like spotting an elusive yellow cardinal singing from my tree, or discovering a shard of turquoise sea glass the size of my thumb in Lake Michigan's surf.

This is the weird way of discipleship.

Eugene Peterson defined *discipleship* as "a long obedience in the same direction."[1] Here, discipleship hinges on enduring proximity, worshipping God, serving our community in joy, sticking around for the long haul, and walking together toward a better way. In practice, it's guaranteed to frustrate, annoy, and inconvenience us. This is sanctification, the wrecking ball and the rebuild. Knowing all this asks of us, do we really want to play a bit role in the discipleship of those near us? Is this slow and hidden work reason enough to endure? And can we possibly begin to see ourselves as among them, modern-day versions of the scrappy, power-grabbing, greedy, disorganized brood of regular men with whom Jesus traveled through life?

White collar, blue collar, no collar at all, there was no rhyme or reason for their thick loyalty to one another. They bickered, shared meals, and probably wore each other's tunics without asking. If their discipleship was anything like the one playing out around me, they bummed a few bucks and didn't pay it back. They spaced birthdays and teased too hard. They cried together and pointed each other toward healing and belief. They hugged it out. They doubted and trusted and, at night, they sat around an open fire and laughed their heads off at the events of the day. They rallied together and took turns doling out the patience of Job.

We're kidding ourselves when we think too formally about our central purpose to reflect God's glory onto those around us. It is in the spoons and forks of everyday living, in the dinner tables and minivans, the text message confessionals and songs we can't help but sing out loud together, that we are drawn to the heart of Christ. He is oxygen. Soil. Sun and rain. He surrounds us, and the narrative uniting us is one in which we constantly take turns pointing. *Here he is!*

Growing hardy roots into the soil of Fifth Street means accepting that people will come and go, and this is neither my fault nor my concern. We will be right here when they need us, easily found. It doesn't matter how much time has passed or how much heartbreak has been dealt. I want them to remember the little white house hugging the curb here on an unspectacular street on the wrong side of the tracks. Most of all, I want them to remember their claim on it, drawn in by the magnetic pull of a God who multiplied dregs into abundance, designed the constellations, and will do whatever it takes to heal us. A wider circle family cannot be chosen, not really. It also can't be abandoned, not really.

Three nights ago, our rowdy crew tromped down the alley in a snowstorm for our Christmas Eve candlelight service. Before I made it into the service, Heather grabbed my arm and stopped me. "Hold on a minute. You gotta see this." She scrolled through her phone for a few seconds, then turned it toward me. "I just had the best day of my life," she said, beaming. There on the screen was a photo of her, her husband, and one of her seven kiddos, a two-year-old with his mama's eyes.

Though custody hasn't yet been returned to her, she's doing the work. She's fighting for their well-being by fighting for her own, clinging to sobriety one day at a time, noticing God's presence in her tiny rental home, surrounding herself with people willing to lace up their gloves on her behalf. "This is the first time we've ever had a picture together with me and his dad sober. I can't stop looking at it." Heaven came down and the whole earth was filled with his wonder. Thousands of years later, in the city of Goshen, the manger miracle was reborn. Jennifer raced off to rehearse with our small church choir, where most of the members are over the age of eighty. I just stood there smiling, glad to be here for the encore.

A thrill of hope.

The weary world rejoices.

———

Five years in, I don't want to guess what any of our friends might have gained by having us around. I can only say that through them we have a truer vision for loyalty and perseverance. Our kinship has shone light on the corners of our faith that had long frustrated us. Drawing near one another with our ordinary lives clanging against theirs, what results is a punchier, jazzier, more wonderfully complex version of ordinary living that glints with the light of the extraordinary.

We're still us. They're still them. A wide conglomeration of quirks and faults. Nothing fancy or dramatic, just the collision of humans doing their level best. Our suffering is now tangled up with their celebration. When they are in pain, we feel the burn. When we're hurting, they hold a cool hand of hope against our foreheads until it seeps beneath our skin. I have acquired a taste for their stripped-down, daily bread faith, far more satisfying than I could have imagined. These days, this is how I'm fed.

Only when discipleship became most vital to my everyday life did I stop to consider how woefully I'd been doing it wrong. It's safe to say our strategy would leave the pillars of many churches swaying precariously with worry. In any case, I'll go ahead and share.

The Martin discipleship MO is heavy on basic togetherness and light on workbooks. I tell people often that I'm
praying for them. I talk to them about my life in the exact way
I would talk to you, my faith a natural, central part of it. Out
of the gates, we don't invite our new friends to church. We
don't lead with pointing out their sin. We don't immediately
tell them their lives would be better with Jesus. We spend time
with them. We give them rides. We watch in awe as our world
is lit by their impossible resilience. They show us the face of
Jesus, tear-tracked and determined.

We tell them, as lavishly as normalcy allows, that God
loves them and created them with a purpose. We tell them
we love them. We find cause to be proud of them (at times
mining great depths for that one true gem) and yammer on
about it well beyond reason. We expose our flaws and look for
opportunities to share our worst failures in order to paint the
clearest picture of God as our escape hatch, saving us more
than once from the brink of ruin.

Paul gave physical shape to the gospel commandment to
love our neighbor broadly and boldly, "knit together by strong
ties of love" (Col. 2:2). "Above all," he wrote, "clothe yourselves
with love" (3:14). To reflect God is to reflect love, so that's where
we begin. God is fierce and powerful. He holds every one of us
in his hand. I can't do any of that, but I can love. Not as well as
he does, not as perfectly or completely, but it's within my job
description to hope for those around me with a fierceness that
radiates into the cold-shocked corners of their hearts, and to
be warmed, in turn, by their hope for me. We stay in such close

proximity that our shoulders can't help but rub, transferring pieces of ourselves—of Christ in us—onto the other. The big work is all his. We're just lucky to feel the temperature rising.

A week ago there was a tap on the door so faint, I almost talked myself out of hearing it at all. On the other side was Jason, the young friend I so often lose sleep over. He's always looking for Cory, but that day, he was willing to settle for me.

We stood on the porch for a couple of minutes struggling through an off-brand of small talk, made difficult due to a slight language barrier, or more likely from the fog of depression and his attempts to self-medicate. My heart lurched into my throat as he looked past me and stared at the street, ready to leave. And that was when the Holy Spirit stood guard on our tiny patio, blocking his exit as I let loose with the discipleship of unforeseen affirmation, cramming in as much as possible before the weight of love would scare him off.

"I ain't used to people saying nice s**t about me," he had told Cory the previous week. We were up for the challenge of changing this.

He didn't break eye contact as tears tracked a course down to his chin, decades of shame splashing onto his bright Nike tennis shoes.

"We love having you around," I said, and I meant it. Stealing a page from Father Greg Boyle's playbook, I reminded him he is exactly who God had in mind when he made him. "Your friends have betrayed you, but maybe this is God having your back. We love you. We're rooting for you. God made you with a purpose, and we'll do whatever it takes to help."

And then he was gone.

When we heard that same quiet knock late on Christmas night, he didn't want to come inside. With a quick hello and a merry Christmas, he hugged Cory before he left and disappeared again. We know we'll see him again soon. He knows where to find us.

I can't scientifically prove that any of this matters. I can't plot his faith journey on a timeline, and I sure can't point to our place in it. Church experts and authors more theologically astute might say this doesn't amount to much or count for anything. *Have you prayed the prayer with him? Has he made a commitment? Are you discipling him?*

All I can tell you is that Jason has been stitched snugly against the interior wall of my heart, along with so many others. His inevitable return is the bloom of discipleship. However long it takes, we will wait here with the good news of his belovedness like a hot cup of coffee on a cold December night. There's simply nothing that can be done about it at this point.

I get twitchy when people make assumptions about my life from a safe distance, glowing or otherwise. The truth, of course, is that I'm a regular woman constantly trying to keep the pull of the world at bay. I love Jesus and prefer my view from his perspective, so I do what I can to yank his eyeglasses. I'm no different than the rest of us, and, at the center of my soul, I trust that, given the chance, most of us would find ourselves smitten by the nourishing love of the neglected people nearby. We come closer, moving past our old judgments and into the space where we understand why Jesus spoke the Beatitudes and stood with the least powerful at every turn. Even better, we experience him in ways that capsize our vision for safety, contentment, and basic, astonishing grace. We keep wanting more, and there's no use fighting it.

This is not about leading my neighbors to Christ. Rather, it's about settling into my truest state of smallness and allowing them to walk me straight to the places where he sits.

My friend Jessica has the sort of kind eyes that make me want to lay my head on her shoulder when I'm having a bad day. She has known the desolate landscape of struggle. Hunger and wanting blow through her life like gale-force winds through a thin cotton jacket. But when she looked at me one evening and said, "We get to be fascinated by God every day," I believed her.

My long obedience is to stay put, a fixed point in a swirling sky, planted here until I'm told otherwise in order to reflect the light that snaps the darkness. This isn't exactly the view of discipleship I was taught, but it's very much the one I'm learning to live, where interruptions happen without warning and where I occasionally find myself dicing potatoes for dinner while praying fervently for the impromptu drug intervention going down a couple streets over for someone we dearly love.

I don't want the old way back. When that friend falls deeper into despair, I want to be sitting on my couch, fielding desperate text messages. I want Cory to hop in his car at ten o'clock at night and drive through the city, trying to hunt him down. I want our prayers for him to be the last thing on our lips as we drift side by side to sleep.

Weeks later, when his eyes are clearer, I want to be there beside him again at church. I want him waving at me from across the street while I'm out running errands. I want him with us on Christmas day.

Discipleship looks like my parents' little country church in the middle of the woods meeting each week to serve the fourteen kids who attend their Awana club. This is no-hype faithfulness, loving people who can't exactly pay them back with no regard for quantifiable growth and no longing to be cool. They show up. They stick around. They trust their long roots will yield fruit.

Discipleship looks like my friend Adam, the founder of a Christian nonprofit formed around mentorship. When the teenagers in his urban Atlanta neighborhood said they needed better schools and committed teachers, he handed over the reins of the nonprofit and went to work as the chemistry teacher at their failing city school. As a result, his flexible schedule has lost its snap. His wife Rebecca now bears a heavier load at their nonprofit, Blueprint 58. In many ways, he's climbing Mt. Everest wearing flip-flops and a lead vest. But these are the ones he loves, and this is what they need. Serving them by the glow of the Bunsen burner probably isn't the ministry he envisioned, but it's essential, and that's enough.

Discipleship looks like my weekly coffee-shop sister, Becca, who surprised herself yet again by taking a part-time position in the new homeless shelter in our city. She called after her shift on Christmas Day saying it was the best Christmas morning she's had in years. "When you spend time with a bunch of people who don't really belong anywhere, and you yourself don't really belong anywhere, you sort of realize you belong to each other."

Just as Jesus instructs us through parables, we lead by our stories. I want the search-party story. The lighthouse story. The living-at-the-end-of-myself story, where I link arms with the ones I love and we stand together, one foot jammed against the cross, the other on the cold, stone floor of the empty tomb. I want a story of beating-heart interdependence with the saints around me, sharpening each other as we walk together through life, every day a bit closer to the heart of our Father.

I want to stay sunk in the story of God, shaping my last splinter of hope into a sturdy lifeboat, a bridge worn smooth by his goodness, a faith that's warp-proof.

This is long-haul discipleship.

This is why we stay.

Chapter Eighteen

Better Homes and Gardens

When we open our lives to those from whom we used to keep a safe distance, it changes everything. Our well-being becomes mashed up with that of our neighbors', and this shifts how we think about our homes, our time, our money, and our ideas about everything from personal responsibility to success. Loving people at close range unveils all we haven't known, the stuff we've gotten wrong for a long time, or maybe forever. Uncomfortable as this can feel, it is exactly what God intended. God uses the people near us to do surgery on our hearts and turn them toward the things that capture his. There should be no segment of life left unscathed by the scalpel of the gospel. The death of self is marked with scars.

For me and my family, the longer we're here in this place of intentional side-by-side living, committed to staying with grit and gusto, the more aware we are of certain gaps in our understanding. One of the most obvious examples was when we woke up to the crisis men and women face after they're released from jail. Though it's hard to imagine, reentry is often more stressful than the incarceration itself. We lived it first with Robert.

The thing you need to know about Robert is that he's charming as all get out. He's funny, witty, and quick to laugh. Also, he's smart and handsome, and, yes, we are biased. Why do you ask? The point is, we weren't prepared for how hard it would be for him to find a job after prison. He had a fresh GED and a million-dollar smile. He had excellent references, a firm handshake, and solid eye contact.

He made the rounds to places within biking distance from our house. Grocery stores, fast-food joints, dishwasher positions. No one called for an interview. Finally, Cory called one of the places on his list and asked what happens when someone checks the felony box on an application. It *said* it doesn't preclude employment, but was that true? The manager laughed. "Yeah, we say it doesn't hurt your chances, but if there are other applicants, we just throw those away."

Eventually Robert settled in at a local factory. Before long, he was ready to move out on his own, opening the window for us to peer at the second hurdle facing the formerly incarcerated poor: safe, affordable housing.

When Cory started working as the chaplain, we saw it on repeat. His friends would be released, often with their self-worth only ankle-high, ready to prove everyone wrong yet terrified of freedom. They'd be overwhelmed with requirements but wouldn't have what they needed to see them through. On top of that, after living in constant community, they'd often find themselves crushed by loneliness. I can't tell you how many times someone has told me they can't sleep once they're out—it's too quiet. Too dark.

Meanwhile, many of them are also fending off addiction. Maybe they're trying to break free of past relationships and realizing how impossible that will be. They ache to rebuild trust with family and their kids, but as they look out at the light of the world, what bounces back at them is the prevailing sense that we're all waiting for them to prove their unworthiness.

It's not unusual for the immense and immediate pressure to kick someone back into a lifestyle of desperation.

Staring straight into the center of this devastating sun, our dreams began to shift. Seven years ago I was dreaming about building a sleeping porch onto the north side of our farmhouse, something like the one in the movie, *The Man in the Moon*. It wasn't enough to hear the frogs croaking from our bedroom windows at night. I wanted to be immersed in them. It wasn't enough that we had six bedrooms. I wanted more.

Now, we sit thigh to thigh with people the world tries to keep down. We fall asleep to the soundtrack of an average day's events—struggle, disruption, beauty. And we want more.

Despite the fact that it felt about as doable as hopping a midnight train to Jupiter, we began to hope for a little house here in our neighborhood that could be a haven for someone in need of a second chance.

Three years after the seed was sown, on my regular morning walk home from school, my eye was drawn to a house I had never noticed, blurring into a block of faded siding and gabled rooflines. The silk daffodil wreath on the screen door drew me in. It spoke my language, the broken down and the lovely. In the face of winter eternal, it screamed promise. In it, I saw my friends. I saw me. I took a picture and kept on walking.

A few months later there was a For Sale sign in the yard.

As it turned out, we were not meant to buy a fixer-upper in our 'hood. The dream was right, but the details were all wrong. Instead, the jail ministry snapped it up, and an entire village of gutsy, optimistic, tenderhearted people laced up their boots and got to work. This dream was never meant to be about us. We don't get ownership of this very good thing. Isn't that lucky? Isn't God gracious to look at our big ideas and say we're dreaming too small when we think we could do it alone?

Night after night, Cory, along with droves of volunteers, tossed their spare time into the bucket, making a home for a family once resigned to a future of slumlords, cockroaches, and cracked window panes.

I put an SOS out to my blog readers— "Help us stock the kitchen!"—and the Amazon wish list was fulfilled in under forty minutes. We kept adding to it, in part because the eventual tenants were starting from scratch, but also because we couldn't bear to turn away generous people with a heart for their neighbor. Maybe they would like a picnic table! Maybe a grill! Who's to say they don't need a rolling pin? A microplane? A vacuum? A bird feeder? A box of tulip bulbs? A tea kettle, for when their friend Shannan comes over?

Two days later, the UPS driver shot me daggers for slowing down his route. We could barely clear a path from our front door to our kitchen, thanks to the towering cardboard boxes. And the gifts kept coming.

A woman I first met at a PTO meeting filled the house's freezer with meat. Someone left a cute little pumpkin on the patio. An online friend crocheted our soon-to-be neighbors an afghan. I spoke at a local church, and a woman I've never met before handed me a houseplant. "A house isn't a home without one of these," she said.

The unbridled enthusiasm surrounding the story God was writing for this family was living proof: we are all longing to be part of something bigger than ourselves. Sometimes we get so hung up on doing something great, we forget the best thing is often the smallest.

Aesop, the ancient Greek storyteller, wrote this eons ago: "No act of kindness, no matter how small, is ever wasted." What makes these simple words even more beautiful is understanding that when we all throw our small stuff together, the pile grows in a flash.

Making the world better for one person makes the world better.

And we can start with whatever we've got.

A friend of Cory's, a dentist in town, keeps outfitting friends of ours with brand-new sets of teeth, completely on the house. (Poverty and drug addiction incite horrors on oral health.) We're constantly sensitive to the fact that he might have reached his capacity with this pro bono work. The last time Cory raised our concerns he smiled and said, "You can't send too many. Keep them coming."

One person at a time, he clears the rubble, restoring dignity in a profoundly personal way, laying another fresh stretch of pavement on the Jericho road for men and women as deserving of kindness and respect as the rest of us.

That's so pointedly how I want to live, seeing my gifts as tools for the kingdom, not to be hoarded or used to seclude myself, but as a basic loaf of bread, meant to be shared.

Isaiah 58, an emotional outline of what God considers true worship, has become one of my favorite chapters in the Bible. I've particularly fallen in love with the middle section.

> The LORD will guide you continually, giving you water when you are dry and restoring your strength. You will be like a well-watered garden, like an ever-flowing spring. Some of you will rebuild the deserted ruins of your cities. Then you will be known as a rebuilder of walls and a restorer of homes. (vv. 11–12)

As we work for the glory of God and his kingdom coming nearer, he's right here, too, with a thermos of ice water. The labor won't be for nothing. Woven into his plan for our redemption, what is broken will be rebuilt and masterfully restored and we will be part of that holy work. I cannot read those verses without choking up.

God doesn't tell us through his prophet Isaiah that we are the workers, tasked with planting a garden. As usual, he flips the grid.

The workers don't plant the garden.

The workers *are* the garden.

We are zinnias and peonies with calloused hands. We cling to him and the garden blooms. Because he is with us, tending to our wounds, being our rest and our strength, we have the endurance to rebuild broken things.

You can't send too many. Keep them coming.

The physical garden in my backyard is child's play compared to the garden we used to have back on the farm. Four raised beds against a gritty backdrop of asbestos-shingled garages, automobile carcasses, and a weed-besieged alley. There's no shade near our garden and it's awfully close to traffic. I never pictured myself with one foot in the street and the other in the beans, calling life from the dirt with a sweaty back. But trying to see the future is overrated here.

Every spring, we suspend our disbelief and push tiny seeds into the dirt. There are always a few good tomatoes, and there are always, always flowers. This is the promise of creation. These are the people we're learning to love. This is us. It's a leap of faith. This was the garden we were given.

We won't begrudge its smallness, because a bloom is a bloom, and just one is miracle enough.

Author Jill Briscoe, after decades of pastoring with her husband of fifty-five years, defined our mission field as the place between our two feet at any given time. She summarized the ministry strategy as this: "Go where you're sent. Stay where you're put. Unpack, as if you're never going to leave. And give what you've got." This is our job. Every day. Until we are told to go, we stay.

A few weekends ago, one of my bonus daughters, Gracie, age five, prayed this before dinner: "God, please turn every garden into Eden." I snapped my eyes open, stunned. I'm not sure I've ever heard a more prophetic word. Few days have passed since that night when I haven't felt their weight.

We are a garden with a job to do, alive with the possibility of all that waits just outside our line of vision. We're invited to stick around for the good stuff, to rebuild lost cities through the hope of the cross.

We get to do this because it has been done for us.

The work is sanctifying, and we can't possibly do it alone.

"Stay here in this land. If you do, I will build you up and not tear you down; I will plant you and not uproot you" (Jer. 42:10).

Wherever you are, you've been planted there with purpose.

Jam your flag into the hard-packed soil and claim it, not for what it is, but for what it will soon be.

Chapter Nineteen

We Bloom

Outside our living room windows stands a hackberry tree, only three years in our soil. I watch it all the time. Its arms have stretched a bit longer while it sleeps through each winter, making good on the promises I occasionally offer my hopped-up kids at bedtime, that growth happens quiet and unnoticed while we sleep.

For months it waits, enduring snow, surviving plows, sleds, and various iterations of a semimotorized snow cart created exclusively for the sloping sidewalk by our own Silas and Ruby Martin. From November to March it serves as our faithful companion, and if that sounds like a load of city-slicker melodrama, please note that my nine-year-old still begins every prayer with, "Dear God, thank you for the trees."

Our sentimental tendencies notwithstanding, the hackberry was not just made to provide visual interest in January, when there's really nothing else to see. It leafs out in April, new life emerging from its throbbing knuckles, the fruit of that hidden winter labor. After surviving a slushy landscape of gray and inelegant sunsets that drop into darkness before dinnertime, we've earned the right to be spellbound by birds and budding trees.

The tree dazzles in October. It shields us in July.

All these things are true, but ultimately, the hackberry tree was made to shelter, to cleanse, to offer respite, to hold things together. Its worship is its life, most ordinary, and we are summoned to live by its example.

The world keeps cranking itself into overdrive, trying hard to give us all the blues. Tonight as I type out these last words to you, my friends in the trenches, we are profoundly at capacity. In the past two days alone, we have clasped hands with friends facing incomprehensible tragedy. This morning, I read a national headline and burst into tears.

But tucked away in my quiet corner, I sat with the windows open, absorbing the white noise of train whistles and rap music as I flipped the pages of Ruth Reichl's *My Kitchen Year*, a book so gorgeous that I took notes with a colored pencil scrounged from the living room floor, mysteriously tied to a ball of yarn.

The evening breeze floated through curtains more beautiful than any curtains deserve to be, and the cat kept me company. Cory ran out to pick up our favorite late-night treat, chips and salsa from a Mexican restaurant here in town while I devoured Ruth's story about loss making way for liberty. She wrote about the world outside her own window, along with morning scones, homemade hummus, crisp-skinned chicken, injury, loneliness, vinegar, and family. She had my whole heart for my whole life, or at least for that one perfect evening.

It was bliss.

I felt immensely lucky in that moment to have both the tension of my everyday life along with sunburned cheeks, a sprawling family tree, and the comfort of a cookbook on my lap on a Saturday night. It's all I never knew to want.

Somewhere around 10:00 p.m., Ruth's artistry nudged me into my kitchen, where pantry staples are reborn. I streamed Sarah McLachlan, Toad the Wet Sprocket, and Nichole Nordeman, and set a place for any emotion that needed a seat.

Moving from the mixer to the island to the soapy water in the sink, my fingertips scented with cardamom pods and orange peel, I thought about how much life had changed, how dramatically the seasons keep rotating, each one jolting my senses, and all I could think was, *I'm still me.*

This world, it will change us in so many uncomfortable, astonishing ways. But we're still here, doing the things we've already done in the hidden corners of our precious, ordinary lives. We're still here in our kitchens. We're still here in our skin. The pain we face might look different now, but so much of life exists just to keep us in place.

We will continue to be bombarded with global crises and national funk, and we need to keep our head in the game. But God did not send his Son to earth as a politician or a nonprofit CEO. He sent our Savior as an everyday man and circled him up with an unlikely chosen few, misfits, regular folks trying to do better, just like us.

Then, as now, he drew mankind's attention down to street level with the divine mission to push back the darkness one small moment at a time. For me, in this year of "Now what?" freedom is the sizzle of peppers hitting a hot skillet. It's yellow cake with salted chocolate ganache. It's walking shoes. A magnifying glass. A broom to sweep up the crumbs.

What I know now is that sometimes the best thing we can do for the world we're in is let our roots keep growing with no regard to the climate around us.

We sleep. We work. We bloom.

We light up the world.

Let me leave you with an Irish blessing that I love:

Deep peace to you:
The deep peace of the quiet earth to you;
The deep peace of the gentle night to you;
The deep peace of the shining stars to you;
The deep peace of Christ the light of the world to you;
The deep peace of God be yours, now and forever.
Amen and amen.

Acknowledgments

Writing *The Ministry of Ordinary Places* has been an exercise in honoring the truth that belonging transforms the world, splashing color onto our everyday and holding us together. God is wildly alive in our midst and in the people around us. I can't stop grinning about it.

To everyone who has asked about my writing, made space for progress, cheered me on and told me to get back to work, thank you. There are too many of you to name, and this book would still be cobwebs if it wasn't for you.

To my neighbors, I knew two years ago that you had already changed my life. Our friendships keep growing richer, locking us in as the crew I didn't even know to hope for. Thank you for accepting me just as I am, for expecting me to show up in my baseball cap and with an undercooked casserole. Thank you for showing me the bright beauty of answering a question with another question and seeing the thread to its end, even when it's 1:00 a.m. and the mosquitoes are biting. Thank you for letting me need you and trusting me to write about it.

Sarah, Kim, Timi, and Megan, you guide me back into

daylight when I go dark for too long. I owe you a debt of optimism and air-time.

Becca and Danielle, you understand the strangest, saddest, funniest details of my ordinary life, proving yourselves the best company here in the wonky land of the living.

To my reader-friends who have followed me across some pretty rugged terrain and over long stretches of boring pavement, it was your faces I saw as I wrote. May our sweaty backs and flat bangs unite us as we trade comfort for the hard work of actual love. Thank you for sticking with me.

Seth Haines, you helped me find the thread and color it gold.

Emily P. Freeman, you walk with me toward my next right thing and don't mind when I stop for photos along the way.

Jessica Wong, during our long telephone conversations as this book slowly took shape I often stared out my living room windows. Somehow, you made me believe what I was seeing, what I was living, was a story worth telling, in all of its dazzling, heartbreaking truth. Thank you for your patience, your intuition, and your kindness.

To my mighty Nelson publishing team, Janene MacIvor, Stephanie Tresner, Sara Broun, Aryn VanDyke, I am constantly aware of the time and effort you pour into me. Thank you for believing in this book. And to Beth Ryan, you put your hand on my shoulder and invited a roomful of people to pray for my neighbors. I tear up just remembering.

Curtis and Karen Yates, it is not enough to call you my agents. You have lit so many lanterns for me and poured buckets of cool water over my worries. Thank you for your protection, your encouragement, your humor, and your trust.

To my launch team, you carried my heart in your hands and made an adventure of something that could have been terrifying. I suppose this is exactly what happens when we belong to each other. Thank you for being funny and smart, for cheering me on always, and for laughing *with* me when I came to you scattered and absurd. I raise my chip (with extra salsa) to each of you!

Mom, Dad, Keisha, and Noal, you always laughed at my stories, so I hold you partly responsible for this unexpected career. Thank you for your love and support along the way. I promise I'll never write about the pickles.

Robert, Calvin, Ruby, and Silas, thank you for choosing me. You are generous, resilient, ridiculous humans. I had no idea our story would unfold quite like this and our life, in so many ways, makes me love being wrong. I would sit by you every day at lunch and play with you at every recess.

Cory, the more we let go, the stronger we become. You absorb my worries and exhaust your (astonishingly low) daily wordcount with me, always. Thank you for helping me hold so many wobbly, sputtering pens. I love you. I can't wait to see what happens next.

Notes

Chapter 1: Who Even *Is* My Neighbor?

1. Martin Luther King, Jr., "I've Been to the Mountaintop" (speech, Memphis, TN, April 3, 1968), transcript from Martin Luther King, Jr., and the Global Freedom Struggle, accessed February 4, 2018, https://kingsinstitute.stanford.edu /encyclopedia/ive-been-mountaintop.

Chapter 2: Locking Eyes with the World We're In

1. Barbara Brown Taylor, *An Altar in the World: Finding the Sacred Beneath Our Feet* (Norwich: Canterbury Press, 2009), 22–23.
2. Brennan Manning and Michael W. Smith, *The Ragamuffin Gospel* (Colorado Springs: Multnomah Publishers, 2000), 24.
3. Eugene H. Peterson, *Under the Unpredictable Plant: An Exploration in Vocational Holiness* (Grand Rapids: William B. Eerdmans Publishing, 1994), 130.

Chapter 3: Speech Therapy for the Common Big Mouth (Like Me)

1. Sara Miles, *City of God: Faith in the Streets* (Nashville: FaithWords, 2014).
2. Henri J. M. Nouwen, *Bread for the Journey: A Daybook of Wisdom and Faith* (New York: HarperCollins, 2006).

Chapter 4: Salted Chocolate

1. Daniel Ritchie, "God Shouts to Us in Our Pain," *Desiring God*, January 16, 2017, https://www.desiringgod.org/articles/god -shouts-to-us-in-our-pain.
2. William Kent Krueger, *Ordinary Grace* (New York: Simon and Schuster, 2014), 195.

Chapter 5: How to Love

1. Justice Conference, Willow Creek Church, June 2017.
2. Gregory Boyle, *Tatoos on the Heart: The Power of Boundless Compassion* (New York: Simon and Schuster, 2011), 136–137.

Chapter 8: Tacos and Tea

1. Jen Hatmaker, *For the Love* (Nashville, TN: Thomas Nelson, 2015), 108–112.

Chapter 9: Searching for Your People

1. Dietrich Bonhoeffer, *The Cost of Discipleship* (New York: Simon and Schuster, 2012), 94.

Chapter 12: Contact Burns

1. Johann Hari, "The Likely Cause of Addiction Has Been Discovered, and It Is Not What You Think," *Huffington Post*, updated April 18, 2017, https://www.huffingtonpost.com /johann-hari/the-real-cause-of-addicti_b_6506936.html.
2. Donald P. McNeill, Douglas A. Morrison, and Henri Nouwen, *Compassion: A Reflection on the Christian Life* (New York: Doubleday, 1982), 25.

Chapter 14: Arms Linked

1. Five (5) states reported male suspension rates higher than the nation for every racial/ethnic group: Florida, Indiana, North

Carolina, Rhode Island, and South Carolina, https://ocrdata
.ed.gov/downloads/crdc-school-discipline-snapshot.pdf.
2. Nell Bernstein, *Burning Down the House: The End of Juvenile Prison* (New York: The New Press, 2014), 259.
3. Helen Prejean, *Dead Man Walking: An Eyewitness Account of the Death Penalty in the United States* (New York: Vintage Books, 1994), 7.

Chapter 15: Redefining Success

1. Charles H. Spurgeon, "The Prayer of Jabez: A Sermon," Christian Classics Ethereal Library, accessed February 4, 2018, https://www.ccel.org/ccel/spurgeon/sermons17.xxvii.html.
2. Edwin Searcy, ed., *Awed to Heaven, Rooted in Earth: Prayers of Walter Brueggemann* (Minneapolis: Fortress Press, 2003).
3. Paul Sparks, Tim Soerens, and Dwight J. Friesen, *The New Parish: How Neighborhood Churches Are Transforming Mission, Discipleship and Community* (Downers Grove, IL: InterVarsity Press, 2014).

Chapter 16: A Theology of Endurance

1. "Dr. Neil-MD," Body Soul Connection, accessed February 4, 2018, http://www.thebodysoulconnection.com/Education Center/fight.html.
2. John Ortberg, "Dallas Willard, a Man from Another 'Time Zone,'" *Christianity Today*, May 8, 2013, http://www .christianitytoday.com/ct/2013/may-web-only/man-from -another-time-zone.html.

Chapter 17: The Discipleship of Sticking Around

1. Eugene Peterson, *A Long Obedience in the Same Direction* (Downers Grove, IL: InterVarsity Press, 2000).

A Personal Note from Shannan Martin

If you lived in my neighborhood, most days you would see me wearing a T-shirt and baseball hat and taking pictures of the sky, the street, or the flowers that spring up between the cracks in the sidewalk. It wouldn't be long before I invited you over for tea or maybe dinner, and chances are, I would be serving tacos spread out haphazardly across the island, along with my award-winning salsa. Amid the dishes in the sink and the kids that would likely be yelling, fighting, or gridlocked in a combination of both, there would be laughter and the sort of conversation that leaves all of us satisfied. If I know anything at all, it's that life is better with the door left open and there is always enough to go around.

On the off-chance that you don't live in Goshen, Indiana, we can still be virtual neighbors!

Walk with me through daily, ordinary life right here:

[instagram] @shannanwrites

[twitter] @shannanwrites

[facebook] @shannanmartinwrites

And be sure to grab my (free!) Neighbor's Manifesto at www.shannanmartinwrites.com.

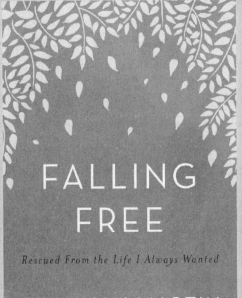

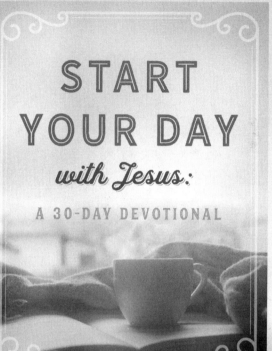

Download this *Free*
30-DAY DEVOTIONAL

START YOUR DAY

with *Jesus:*

A 30-DAY DEVOTIONAL